MW01491989

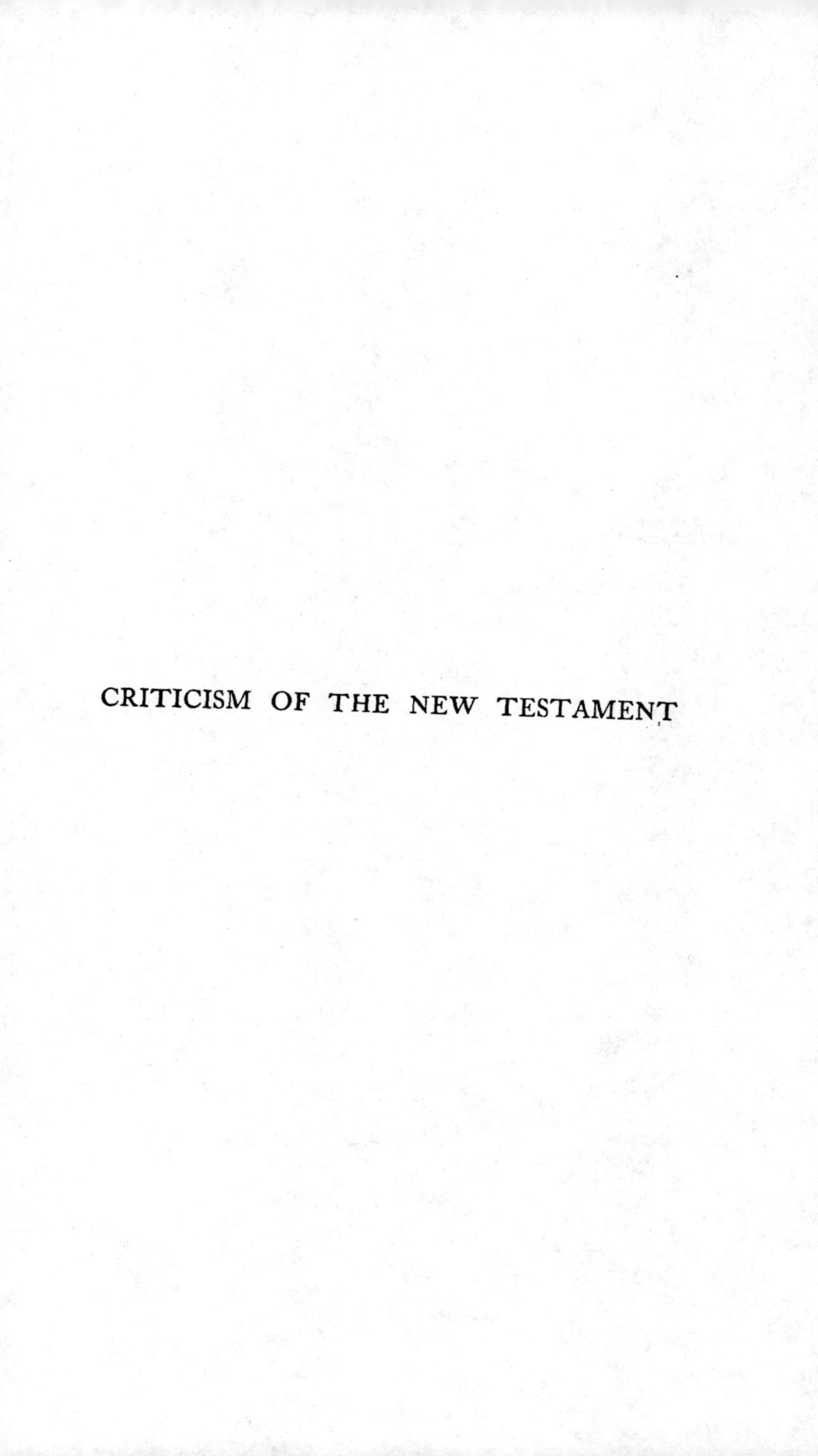

CRITICISM OF THE NEW TESTAMENT

CRITICISM OF THE NEW TESTAMENT

ST. MARGARET'S LECTURES

1902

BY

W. SANDAY, D.D.

F. G. KENYON, D.Litt., Ph.D.

F. C. BURKITT, M.A.

F. H. CHASE, D.D.

A. C. HEADLAM, B.D.

J. H. BERNARD, D.D.

Wipf and Stock Publishers
199 West 8th Avenue, Suite 3
Eugene, Oregon 97401

Criticism of the New Testament
St. Margaret's Lectures, 1902
By Sanday, William, Kenyon, Frederick, Burkitt, F. C., Headlam, A. C.,
Chase, F. H. and Bernhard, J. H.
ISBN: 1-59244-492-X
Publication date 1/26/2004
Previously published by John Murray, 1902

Prefatory Note

THE condition of sound interpretation of Scripture is honest and thorough criticism. Ultimately all our theological and ecclesiastical discussions turn on the treatment of the sacred text, and it is beyond question that within the last two generations the traditional treatment has been to an extent which is difficult to exaggerate disallowed. Much of our standard theological literature is practically worthless because based on a discarded exegesis; and it is humiliating to reflect that much current preaching and teaching of religion is only tolerated because the religious public remains extraordinarily ignorant of the assured results of Biblical Science. In the prevailing ignorance unwarrantable fears invade the general mind, and create a panic-stricken prejudice against critical studies, eminently favourable to that resuscitation of fanaticism which is one of the most curious and melancholy characteristics of our time. It becomes therefore a matter of no slight importance that sound knowledge as to the methods and conclusions of criticism should be disseminated as widely as possible among the people. The lectures here printed were designed as a first step in a serious effort to awaken popular interest in Biblical Science, and to set out clearly the broad principles on which that criticism proceeds. Of course only the fringe of the subject is here touched. The names of the lecturers will sufficiently commend their work to all who have any acquaintance with the world of contemporary scholarship. Without exception they speak with the authority of recognized experts. I may be permitted to set on record my cordial thanks for the ready kindness with which they consented to co-operate with me in an undertaking, which, apart from them, I should have been powerless to carry through. The famous and beautiful Church of S. Margaret, Westminster, is, in many notable respects, well suited to be a teaching-centre of that New Learning, which is slowly but surely revolutionizing Christian thought. I have always felt that the critical results, secured by the labours of scholars in the Universities, ought to be more directly, and, so to speak, naturally communicated to the Church at large, and given their proper effect in the current doctrine and worship. There are many educated laymen, who have no time for reading elaborate works, and whose lack of acquaintance with the technicalities of criticism makes such works uninteresting and even unintelligible, who yet are keenly interested in the honest treatment of Scripture, and fully able to appreciate critical methods and results when these are set before them with reasonable lucidity. No worse disaster to religion could well be imagined than the divorce of critical scholarship from average belief. Criticism must not be allowed to take an esoteric character, but, at all hazards, must be held closely to the current teaching of the Church. These lectures will have justified their publication, and answered to the purpose with which they were originally planned, if, in however small a measure, they contribute to this end.

It is requisite that I should state clearly that every lecturer's responsibility is strictly confined to his own contribution, and that I myself must answer for the plan of the lectures and the choice of subjects and lecturers.

H. HENSLEY HENSON.

WESTMINSTER, *August*, 1902.

Contents

PAGE

INTRODUCTORY LECTURE: THE CRITICISM OF THE NEW TESTAMENT, - - - - - - 1

By PROFESSOR W. SANDAY, D.D., Canon of Christ Church, Oxford; Lady Margaret Professor of Divinity in the University of Oxford.

MANUSCRIPTS, - - - - - - - - 31

By F. G. KENYON, D.Litt., Ph.D., Assistant Keeper of MSS., British Museum.

THE ANCIENT VERSIONS OF THE NEW TESTAMENT, 68

By F. C. BURKITT, M.A., Trin. Coll., Camb.

THE HISTORY OF THE CANON OF THE NEW TESTAMENT, - - - - - - 96

By PROFESSOR F. H. CHASE, D.D., President of Queen's College, Cambridge.

THE DATES OF THE NEW TESTAMENT BOOKS, - 145

By REV. A. C. HEADLAM, B.D., Rector of Welwyn.

THE HISTORICAL VALUE OF THE ACTS OF THE APOSTLES, - - - - - - - - 208

By J. H. BERNARD, D.D., Trinity College, Dublin, Dean of St. Patrick's Cathedral, Dublin.

The
Criticism of the New Testament

The Criticism of any work of antiquity has two branches, which are commonly distinguished as the Lower Criticism and the Higher.

The Lower Criticism deals with the smaller questions of words and text. Its problem is to determine as nearly as may be what the author really wrote.

The Higher Criticism deals with the larger questions of authorship, date, sources, composition, literary and historical character. Its problem is to set the writing in its place among other writings; to determine where it comes in place and time and what are its relations, internal and external: I mean what are the relations of the parts that compose it to the whole, and what are the relations both of the parts and of the whole to the surrounding literature and history, *i.e.* broadly to the intellectual, and in the case of the N.T., to the religious conditions of the time.

These two groups of questions mark respectively the spheres of the Lower and of the Higher Criticism.

The names are not altogether fortunate. They have lent themselves to a rather natural misuse and misunderstanding.

It is obvious to take the Lower Criticism as meaning the inferior, and the Higher as meaning the superior branch of the science. The Lower Criticism is apt to seem a work of drudgery. And it is possible to discern sometimes in the Higher Critic just a shade of self-complacency, as though he were in possession of a mystery not to be shared with the profane crowd. And where the critic does not make this assumption for himself the outside world is apt to make it for him. It is better to dismiss any such associations as these, and to treat the two departments as being what they are, simply two branches of one science that come into the day's work each in its turn.

My duty on the present occasion is, not to go into any details, which will be dealt with by my successors, but to describe to you as shortly and as broadly as I can the main problems and the present position, first of the Lower and then of the Higher Criticism of the New Testament.

It is well at the outset that you should realize the extraordinary intricacy and subtlety of the questions arising under each of these heads, but especially under the first.

No other book comes anywhere near the N.T. in the extent, the variety, and the excellence of the evidence of its text.

The Greek MSS. alone are said to number some three thousand. Some of these go back to the fourth, fifth, and sixth centuries of our era: one recently-discovered fragment is said to be even as old as the third.

Then there is a series of very ancient and important versions, each with a number, and some with a very great number of MSS. of its own.

Besides these, there is the almost inexhaustible field of Patristic quotations in Greek and Latin which render valuable aid in determining the text.

Two ancient authors, Homer and Virgil, have MSS. (in the first case only fragments) as old, or even older than the MSS. of the N.T. And for these poems, quotations, and the writings of early grammarians supply material of value. But the limits of variation in verse are less than those in prose; and the N.T., from the peculiar circumstances of its early transmission, is exceptional among prose writings. The text of Virgil has been well preserved, and presents few difficulties;

while the chief of those which beset the text of Homer go back behind the MS. tradition.

The real problem of the text of the N.T. has a parallel only in the case of the O.T., and that is in some important respects different.

It has come to be understood that the only way of approaching a problem of this magnitude and complexity is by first seeking to recover the history of the text that has passed through so many vicissitudes. For this purpose direct historical statements help us but little, and we are thrown back upon critical analysis—a process which is itself subtle and complex in proportion to the extent of the field which it covers and the multitude of documents which it includes.

The first writers to grapple with this problem of recovering the history of the N.T. text at close quarters and in its full extent were the two Cambridge scholars, Westcott and Hort. Of course they had predecessors, more particularly Griesbach and Lachmann; and the materials on which they worked were contributed mainly by others (especially Tischendorf and Tregelles). But no one before them had confronted the problem with the same penetration and breadth of view. The two volumes of introduction published in the same year as the Revised Version (1881) were an heroic achievement, the greatest single achievement that

English theological science has to show in the century now past. It was a complete science in itself, built up from the very foundation. Ten years ago the text and system of Westcott and Hort seemed to be in full possession of the field. It had of course opponents, but no serious rivals. To-day the situation is different. Still we may say that there is no fully elaborated system to compare with theirs; but important discoveries have been made which are thought in some quarters, and those not the least scientific, to affect the balance of the evidence as they had left it. There is a spirit of enterprise and experiment abroad, which has nowhere as yet attained mature results, but which is actively at work, and the success of which remains to be seen.

Westcott and Hort had made it clear that the two oldest families of texts are that which they called Neutral and that which they called Western. The Neutral is in the main the text of the two oldest (*i.e.* fourth century) MSS., the Vatican and the Sinaitic. The Western is the text mainly represented by the Latin Version, but really diffused throughout the Christian world.

It is to this latter type of text that recent discoveries have made the most marked additions. The Sinai Syriac, brought to light by Mrs. Lewis and Mrs. Gibson, is a text of first-rate importance.

It has stimulated the hope that a comparison of the oldest forms of the Syriac Version with the oldest forms of the Latin may reveal a text worthy to be put in competition with that of the famous Greek uncials.

It is in this shape that I should like to state the problem, as it appears to me to show the greatest promise. An accomplished classical scholar, Dr. Blass of Jena, has worked out a theory with much ingenuity, which, however, I do not think will permanently hold its ground. He would make the two competing texts in the most conspicuous instances represent different editions, both proceeding from the hands of the original author. It is true that we can trace up the types nearly to the time when the writings were composed; but there is still a gap to be bridged, and Dr. Blass' methods of reconstructing his text seem to me open to some exception. My successors perhaps will treat of these issues more in detail.

The most interesting textual questions are concerned with the Gospels and Acts. Questions of a similar kind arise specially in connection with the Pauline Epistles; but here they are less important.

We may congratulate ourselves on the appearance within the last few weeks of a *Handbook to the Textual Criticism of New Testament*, which is quite a model of its kind. Not only does the writer, Mr. F. G. Kenyon, of the British Museum, give an account of the materials of Textual Criticism, which is remarkably full, accurate, and readable, but his whole attitude towards the principles and methods of the science is, I believe, the very best possible. Mr. Kenyon's book brings English scholarship once more to the front in this branch of the subject.[1]

For the general public the questions of the Higher Criticism must have a greater interest than those of the Lower. They are less technical and they touch points of greater moment. For whatever the results of the Lower Criticism may be, they are not likely to touch anything that is vital. Only a small proportion of the various readings that come in question affect in any degree significant points of doctrine or of practice.

But, when we pass over to the Higher Criticism, the case is altered. Here far larger interests are at stake. Questions of date and authorship that might be indifferent in themselves become serious through the facts which depend upon them. We say that Christianity is a historical religion. That

---

[1] Other books that may be recommended are Nestles's *Introduction to the Textual Criticism of N.T.* (E. T., 1901), the new edition of Mr. Hammond's *Outlines* (1902), and a useful little *Primer* by Mr. K. Lake (1900).

means that it rests, to a large extent, on historical evidence; and it is the function of the Higher Criticism to determine the exact nature and weight of that evidence.

For this reason, the process is felt to be one of no light responsibility. There is no other field in which hasty theories or conclusions are more to be deprecated. The unsettling effect of such theories is often out of all proportion to the solidity of the grounds on which they are based.

It should be said frankly that those who are engaged upon the criticism of the N.T. in this country are agreed in the principle that it must be approached "like any other book." Their position is, that if they would discover in what the N.T. differs from other books they must begin by making no exceptions, but applying to it the same methods that they would apply to them.

Sometimes English critics are taunted with not doing this. But the taunt is not well founded. From a rather wide acquaintance with those who are employed in this work, I can take it upon myself to say that they have an absolutely sincere and honest intention to look the facts in the face as they are. If they can be shown to depart from this principle, they would be the first to acknowledge their fault.

There are, however, just two reservations that

they think it right to make. To one of these I have already alluded, viz., that, in view of the importance of the subject, they think it specially incumbent upon them to proceed with great care and caution, embracing, as far as they can, all the facts, and rigorously testing each step before they go on to another.

And the other reservation is, that, if they make no assumptions in favour of the Christian tradition, they also refuse to make any assumptions against it. In other words, they refuse to put a document out of court simply because it contains the miraculous. As this is the very element that they wish to probe to the bottom, and to discover its full significance, they feel it their duty not to prejudge the case against it. There are abundant indications of other kinds by which they can test the literary relations of a writing without reference to this question of the supernatural ; and, therefore, they prefer to leave this till the last, when the strictly literary criteria have had full weight allowed to them. There is scope enough in the N.T. for the Higher Criticism, properly so called, going its own way, and following its own methods and its own laws.

Each section of the Sacred Volume has its own peculiar problems, many of them of great perplexity; so that, in spite of the immense labour expended upon them, there are still many on which there is not as yet any clear agreement.

I will go rapidly through the N.T. section by section, trying to show what are the main issues, and how they arise, endeavouring also to give you some idea of their present position.

It should be distinctly understood that the questions raised—at least those on which I shall touch—are real questions, and are not wantonly invented. They demand an answer; and criticism is doing its best to answer them. For this it should not be condemned, even though some of the hypotheses employed should seem far-fetched and complicated. Complex facts require what will seem to be complicated hypotheses. And although the effort is always after simplicity, there are some solutions that cannot be simple. It is easy to cut the knot, but not so easy to untie it. Much patience therefore is needed—patience on the part of the critic and patience also on the part of the public that judges of his criticism.

That which makes the first three Gospels stand out as a group unique in literature is the extraordinary relation between them at once of close verbal resemblance and of marked difference. If either of these phenomena stood alone, we should have no great difficulty. If we took the resemblances, it would be easy to say either that the three Gospels were copied from or based freely upon one another (*e.g.* St. Matthew following in the steps of St. Mark, and St. Luke following upon St. Matthew), or that they were all three based upon a common original. But then there come in the differences; and it is asked how are we to account for these?

There have always been some, but there are probably fewer at this moment than at any time previously, who have held, or hold, that the peculiar relations in which the Gospels stand to one another are to be explained by oral tradition. They think that nothing was written until we come to the Gospels as we have them, but that the resemblances are caused by the way in which the narrative was committed to memory and repeated by the different narrators to a large extent in the same words. This view had the high authority of the late Bishop Westcott.

It is, however, held now quite by a minority, and even a small minority. Most scholars think that the resemblances are too close to be explained in this way.

The same large majority are agreed in holding that the three Gospels are really based on a common original which very nearly coincided with our present St. Mark.

I say "very nearly coincided"—nearly but not quite. And in that distinction lies the delicacy of the problem and the necessity for theories that may seem to be fine-spun.

I must not go into these; but speaking broadly it may be said that on what is called "the priority of St. Mark" there is an imposing amount of agreement among scholars of all nationalities. If any one wants to know the oldest form in which a complete Gospel narrative was drawn up he has only to read our present St. Mark, all but the last twelve verses, which have a history of their own.

That is the first document. Then there is also considerable agreement in the view that there was a second primitive document, to which perhaps only two out of the three Evangelists had access, but which in any case was most largely used in the First Gospel and the Third. This document would include the common matter, which is mostly discourse, in St. Matthew and St. Luke.

Taken together these two assumptions, of the priority of St. Mark, and a second source consisting mainly of discourse, constitute what is known as the Two-Document Hypothesis.

It has the advantage that it corresponds roughly to a statement by a very early writer called Papias in regard to the Gospels—a statement probably going back to the first decade of the second century.

This Two-Document Hypothesis is at the present moment more largely accepted than any other, though it is right to say that the second half of the hypothesis is not quite so generally accepted as the first ; and among the dissentients are some whose opinions deserve attention.

The principal difficulty in regard to the second document is, that of the passages that would naturally be referred to it some are so much closer in their wording than others. Some sections of the common matter in St. Matthew and St. Luke are almost *verbatim* the same, whereas others are widely divergent. It is not surprising that the question should be asked how it is possible to refer these to one and the same document? Perhaps this difficulty may be removed by a further hypothesis which is finding favour in some quarters, viz., that besides the second document, commonly called the *Logia* or *Oracles*, St. Luke has also a special document of his own, which in part overlapped the *Logia*. The theory is that for some reason, probably derived from the way in which it reached him, St. Luke attached a special weight to this document and, where it contained the same matter as the *Logia*, preferred its wording. Besides a part of the common matter in St. Matthew and St. Luke, this special source would include that group of parables in chapters x.-xviii. which give such a distinctive character to the Third Gospel.

It may be said that average opinion, agreeing in this with an ancient statement in Irenaeus, would place the composition of the first three Gospels within the twenty years 60–80 A.D.

In regard to the Fourth Gospel, although there has been some approximation between the opposing views, and although even in their more extreme forms these are not so widely removed as they were, there is still a rather sharp opposition.

The great question arises from the comparison of this Gospel with the other three.

Now it is of interest to note that the ancients, as well as the moderns, made this comparison and observed the differences which it brought out. I do not mean that they observed all the minute differences of which we are conscious, but broadly speaking they were aware of the facts, and they had their own way of accounting for them.

According to them St. John had the other Gospels brought to him and approved them, adding his own testimony to their truth; but that he noticed an omission of some things, more particularly at the beginning of our Lord's public ministry. They said that, at the instance of the disciples by whom he was surrounded, he undertook in part to supply this omission and at the same time to write a Gospel which should lay more stress upon the Divine side of the history, the human side having been sufficiently treated. As Clement of Alexandria puts it, writing about the year 200 A.D.: "Last of all John, perceiving that the bodily [or external] facts had been made plain in the Gospels, being urged by his friends, and inspired by the Spirit, composed a spiritual Gospel."[1]

In other words the ancients held that the deliberate object of the author of the Fourth Gospel was to supplement the other three.

As a matter of fact this is just what it does. It supplements the other Gospels both as to time and as to place. The ancients noticed that whereas the other Gospels began their main account of the public ministry from the imprisonment of John the Baptist, the Fourth Gospel records a number of events before John was cast into prison. And again, whereas in the other Gospels our Lord's ministry was almost confined to Galilee, St. John alone gives considerable space to events that occurred at Jerusalem. It is coming to be seen that the events of the Last Week imply that our Lord did not then come to Jerusalem for the first time. Both the enthusiasm with which He was welcomed and the

---

[1] Eus. *H.E.*, vi. xiv.

animosity against Him require previous visits to account for them. So that this supplemental matter is rather in favour of St. John's narrative than in any way adverse to it.

But no doubt the main point is that which Clement of Alexandria had in his mind when he spoke of St. John's as a "spiritual gospel." This agrees with what St. John himself meant when he wrote: "These [things] are written that ye may believe that Jesus is the Christ, the Son of God; and that believing ye may have life in His Name."[1] It was his object to bring out the Divine side of the history; he had felt the power of that side himself, and he desired that others should feel it.

All this we may distinctly recognise. When it is said that the picture in the Fourth Gospel is a one-sided picture, we admit that it is. The Evangelist singles out one set of facts to put prominently forward. This is just the intention which Clement ascribed to him. He saw that one side of things had been sufficiently narrated, and he set himself to do fuller justice to the other.

The picture in the Fourth Gospel supplements that in the other three; but does it in any way contradict it? I do not think it does. We might describe the teaching of the Fourth Gospel

[1] John xx. 31.

as a series of variations upon the one theme which has its classical expression in a verse of the Synoptics. "All things have been delivered unto me of my Father: and no one knoweth the Son, save the Father; neither doth any know the Father, save the Son, and he to whomsoever the Son willeth to reveal Him."[1]

St. John is constantly playing round and setting in new lights the filial relation of the Son to the Father. But that relation is really the key, not to his Gospel alone, but to all the four; and indeed we may say not to the Gospels alone, but to the whole of Christianity.

I doubt if it would be easy to suggest a better summary of the mental attitude of the author of the Fourth Gospel than is contained in Browning's lines:

"I never thought to call down fire on such

. . . .

But patient stated much of the Lord's life
Forgotten or misdelivered, and let it work:
Since much that at the first, in deed and word,
Lay simply and sufficiently exposed,
Had grown (or else my soul was grown to match,
Fed through such years, familiar with such light,
Guarded and guided still to see and speak)
Of new significance and fresh result;
What first were guessed as points, I now knew stars,
And named them in the Gospel I have writ."[2]

---

[1] St. Matt. xi. 27.

[2] *A Death in the Desert.*

It is just that. The Evangelist had learnt by reflexion and experience that what he had recognised as "points," as simple facts, were really something more; they were luminous points, or "stars."

The Book of the Acts is a continuation of the Third Gospel, and it is probable, that like the Gospel, it is composite, or at least that to some extent older sources, written or oral, lie behind it. Here, however, we have no longer the advantage of being able to compare other texts, and with their help to define or discriminate these sources. An interesting theory has been put forward, that the document which served as a foundation for the first twelve chapters originally formed part of the special source of the Gospel. If this were so it would not only be the oldest bit of continuous Church History that we can trace, but it will have suggested to St. Luke the idea of following up his first volume by a second. Some attempt has been made to test this theory by a careful examination of the language of chapters i.-xii. compared with that of the supposed "Special Source" of the Gospel. But as yet the theory can hardly be said to be either proved or disproved.

The critical question that is most important for an estimate of the whole book is that which is concerned with the later chapters.

One of the first and most elementary lessons in N. T. criticism will have been suggested to most of us by what are called the "We-passages," *i.e.* those passages in the later chapters of the Acts in which the writer speaks in the first person plural, as though he were himself included in the party whose travels and adventures he is narrating. Was the author of the Acts really himself one of these companions of St. Paul or is he incorporating in his book what may be called a diary written by some one else who had been such a companion?

English scholars generally have been of opinion that the first of these hypotheses explains the facts in the way that is simplest and best. In this instance the criterion of language can be applied more effectively than in the case of the earlier chapters. And I would commend to your notice especially the severely statistical argument in Sir John Hawkins' *Horae Synopticae*, pp. 148-154, which leads to the conclusion that "the original writer of these sections was the same person as the main author of the Acts and of the Third Gospel, and consequently, that the date of those books lies within the lifetime of a companion of St. Paul."

In keeping with this conclusion English scholars have also as a rule attached a high degree of value to the historical narrative of the Acts. This is equally true of Bishop Lightfoot,[1] Professor Ramsay,[2] Mr. Headlam,[3] Dr. Knowling,[4] and of the two most recent writers, Mr. Rackham,[5] and Dr. Chase.[6] There is some exception in Prof. P. Gardner's *Historic View of the New Testament*; but Dr. Gardner's disparagement is only an echo of certain foreign writers and is not supported by argument. There is more argumentative basis for the destructive criticism of Prof. Schmiedel in *Encyclopaedia Biblica*, on which reference may be made to the *Church Quarterly Review* for October, 1901.

The external evidence for the Epistles of St. Paul is very strong. It goes to show not only that individual epistles existed, but that the whole body of thirteen epistles had been already collected about the year 110 A.D. Still, there is a real problem in connexion with these epistles, which

---

[1] Art. "Acts" in Smith's *Dict. of the Bible* (ed. 2, 1893).

[2] *St. Paul the Traveller and the Roman Citizen* (London, 1895).

[3] Art. "Acts" in Hastings' *Dict. of the Bible* (Edinburgh, 1898).

[4] In the *Expositors' Greek Testament*, vol. ii. (London, 1900).

[5] *The Acts of the Apostles.* An Exposition by R. B. Rackham (London, 1901).

[6] *The Credibility of the Book of the Acts of the Apostles* by F. H. Chase (London, 1902).

justifies to some extent the questions that have been raised.

The Epistles of St. Paul fall into four clearly marked groups: (1) A preliminary group containing 1 and 2 Thessalonians; (2) a central group, 1 and 2 Corinthians, Galatians, Romans; (3) the Epistles of the Imprisonment, Ephesians, Colossians, Philippians, Philemon; (4) the Pastoral Epistles, 1 and 2 Timothy, and Titus.

Now it is true that if a literary critic were to compare these groups together, he would soon discover certain differences between them. He would find in them differences both of style and of subject matter. The epistles of the central group have certain marked characteristics. They are controversial; and the controversies with which they deal are conducted with great vivacity of expression, and with rapid changes ot tone and manner. Sharp dialectic, stern denunciation, and affectionate entreaty alternate with each other in rapid succession. The sentences are frequently short, and couched in the form of challenge. They give the impression of a temperament keenly sensitive, quickly roused and as quickly subsiding; of great powers of mind, applied in the most varied directions; of profound thoughts combined with soaring aspirations.

When we turn to an epistle like the Ephesians

it is impossible not to feel a difference. The profundity is there ; the aspiration is there ; but the controversy seems to be in the background. With it the old vivacity appears to be lost. The sentences and paragraphs become longer and more involved. The tone of challenge dies out. Even the affectionateness seems buried in weighty but almost laboured disquisition.

Along with this difference of style the subject matter also appears to change. We hear less of the law, of circumcision, of Christian liberty, and the struggles of the sin-burdened conscience. The leading thought is now that of the Church as the Body of Christ, and of Christ as the Head of the Church.

Again, when we pass on to the Pastoral Epistles, here too there appears to be a change. The number of peculiar words not used by St. Paul elsewhere increases; and the exposition of doctrine gives place to details of ecclesiastical discipline and practical organization.

All these things together make up a real problem at which students of more conservative and of more liberal tendencies have worked side by side.

It has been observed in mitigation of the apparent contrast—

(i.) That although there is a certain change of

subject in the later letters as compared with the earlier, there is never any real inconsistency; the germs of the later teaching are always to be found, and are often expressed very distinctly, at the earlier stages. The development can be shown to be easy and natural; and it is always development, not contradiction.

(ii.) Not only are the changes such as might naturally take place in the same mind, but they are also such as would inevitably arise out of the course of events and through the shifting of circumstances. The great controversy as to circumcision rapidly reached its climax and rapidly died down. The reconciliation of Jew and Gentile was becoming daily an accomplished fact. The Apostle, sensitive to every movement within his little world, felt the progress that was being made and, like the statesman that he was, lost no time in taking advantage of it, to consolidate the advance by constructive doctrine. The teaching of Ephesians and Colossians only marks the phase which naturally succeeded to that of Romans and 1 and 2 Corinthians. And in like manner the peculiarity of the Pastoral Epistles arose out of the situation to which they belonged. There is not a single Epistle or group of Epistles that is not connected by manifold links of connexion with those which had gone before.

(iii.) In regard to style it must be remembered that St. Paul was a genius of extraordinary versatility. The differences of tone and structure between the Epistles of one group and those of another is not greater than that between different portions of the same Epistle and of the same group. We must allow for the fluctuations and oscillations of a mind at once of remarkable sensitiveness and remarkable range. St. Paul was a whole man; the emotional side of his nature was as strong and as active as the intellectual, and the spiritual dominated over both.

(iv.) St. Paul lived intensely, but more intensely at some times than at others. A nature like his implies a highly strung nervous organization. Such a temperament has its ebbs and its flows, to which physical conditions would contribute not a little. It would be one thing to be moving about freely from place to place, in daily intercourse with the brethren, hearing their wants, entering into their disputes, and seeing their dangers,—and a wholly different thing to be living in confinement, actually chained to a Roman soldier, and with only distant echoes of what was going on in the Christian world borne to him from without. It is not really surprising that in the Epistles of the Imprisonment, the currents of the blood and of the brain should seem more torpid than in the rest. Neither is it surprising that the pressing controversy and stirring human interests of the Central group should be reflected in a style more passionate and accentuated than the Apostle's wont. Bishop Lightfoot has somewhere pointed out that we make a mistake in taking these Epistles as a standard of St. Paul's normal habit of writing; he thought that for this purpose the two Epistles to the Thessalonians were better suited.

Following such lines of argument as these the great majority of English scholars have satisfied themselves that although there are these differences between the groups, it is still more than possible that the Epistles are all by the same hand, and that St. Paul's. The differences are not to be overlooked, but they cast an interesting light upon the successive phases of the intense and strenuous life of the great Apostle.

In Germany, too, there has been a steady reaction from the extreme scepticism of the middle of the last century; so that at the present time Harnack accepts ten of the thirteen Epistles, and only makes the reserve that in the case of the Pastorals materials taken from genuine letters of St. Paul have been enlarged and expanded into their present form. The other Epistles that are most questioned are Ephesians and 2 Thessalonians.

The Epistle to the Hebrews stands rather by

itself. The main critical question in regard to it—that as to its authorship—has made but little progress since it was discussed by the scholars of the end of the second and the third centuries, Clement of Alexandria, Origen, and Tertullian. Then, as now, it was agreed that the writer was some one allied in spirit to St. Paul, but the best opinion was that he was not St. Paul himself: according to Clement some said that the Epistle received its actual wording from St. Luke, others from his own namesake, the Roman, Clement. Tertullian alone states positively, as if from knowledge, that the Epistle was the work of Barnabas. Origen says that "who actually wrote it God alone knows." Since that date the only plausible suggestion that has been made is Luther's of Apollos; and now quite recently Harnack[1] has thrown out the idea that it may be the work of the pair, Aquila and Prisca or Priscilla, and more particularly of the latter. This too will seem to be a mere guess, but it is at least supported with much skill.

The question as to the authorship of the Epistle is closely bound up with that as to its address; and the question as to the address turns very much upon the observation which has gained strength in recent years, that the indications in the Epistle

[1] In the new *Zeitschrift für die Neutest. Wissenschaft*, i. 16 ff. (1900).

do not point to any large church or group of churches (such as the churches of Palestine), but rather to some small community like those which are described as meeting "in the houses" of the wealthier Christians. Just such a community met in the house of Prisca and Aquila (Rom. xvi. 5, 1 Cor. xvi. 19); and the personal greetings and very individual allusions look as if they might have been meant for a gathering of this kind. The leading German scholars at the present moment would seek the destination of the Epistle in Rome.

The different constituents of the group of Catholic Epistles stand upon a different footing. It is well known that the books for which there is the oldest evidence are 1 St. Peter and 1 St. John. The criticism of the Epistles of St. John is naturally bound up with that of the Gospel. The most interesting question raised by any member of the group is perhaps that as to 1 St. Peter, how on the supposition of its genuineness we are to account for the relation in which it stands to the teaching of St. Paul. It is now generally agreed that the Epistle shows marked signs of Pauline influence. On this question—and indeed on all points relating to the Epistle—I should like especially to commend to you the commentary recently published on the two Epistles of St. Peter and St. Jude by Dr. Bigg.[1] On all the problems both of criticism and of interpretation, it is written with much freshness and independence, not at all in the groove of any particular school, and with a lively sense of what is natural and human. Dr. Bigg states in an attractive way the view, which is also adopted by Zahn, that Silvanus acted as the amanuensis of St. Peter, and that the latter owed not a little of its actual shape to him. In any case, we may think of Silvanus as a living link between the two Apostles.

Side by side with Dr. Bigg's commentary are the two elaborate and even exhaustive articles by Dr. Chase on the two Epistles that bear the name of St. Peter in Hastings' *Dictionary*. A comparison of these articles with the commentary will place the reader in a good position for forming his own conclusions.

I hesitate rather to speak about the Book of Revelation, of which I have not made any recent study, and in regard to which the critical problems are so complex that no one who has not given them close study should pronounce upon them. If, however, I may give such impression as I have for what it is worth I might almost do so in

[1] In the series of *International Critical Commentaries* : Edinb., 1901.

words recently used by my friend, Dr. Robertson of King's College. "The difficulty of reconciling the indications which point respectively to the Neronic or Domitian dates may be due to the use by the seer, writing under Domitian, of earlier materials. This is too thoroughly in keeping with the phenomena of apocalyptic literature to be set aside as very improbable. But the book as it stands is too entirely the work of its final author to encourage us to hope that the derivative passages can be disengaged with any certainty from their present context. In particular, the hypothesis of a non-Christian Jewish original document appears quite gratuitous. Nor can it be said that the Neronic date for the whole book, in spite of the present tendency to revert to the tradition of Irenaeus, is wholly out of court."[1]

I am inclined to agree with this estimate even in the points in which it deviates somewhat from that which would be held by many scholars, except that I am not quite so sure that the hypothesis of the use of non-Christian materials is wholly to be excluded.

The rapid survey that I have been taking has to do with the Literary Criticism of the N.T., and more particularly with so much of it as

[1] *Regnum Dei;* the Bampton Lectures for 1901, p. 107 n.

English theologians have had no difficulty in recognising. So far as this literary side of criticism is concerned the century which has now elapsed has seen a substantial advance. Many extravagant theories, put forward by way of experiment, have been discarded, and other sounder theories have taken their place. The advance, if slow, has been sure; because it has been accompanied by much careful testing and sifting. The amount of agreement among scholars of different nationalities is increasing, and a reasonable spirit on the whole prevails.

I do not mean that there are not many serious questions still remaining, but those questions are, to a comparatively small extent, literary. Within the region of literary criticism there is enough common ground to make the conflicting opinions no longer, as they at one time seemed, irreconcilable.

The criticism that lies outside the literary sphere is at the present moment rather in a state of flux. Neither the questions to be asked nor the answers to them stand out as yet with sufficient clearness. It would be better that the professed scholars should work at it a little more before it is brought down into the public arena.

Manuscripts

THE criticism of the New Testament, as of any work of literature of sufficient importance to be criticised, falls, according to a common division, into two parts, the higher and the lower criticism. The higher criticism, as is explained more fully in the previous lecture, deals with the origin, history, character, and sources of the books in question; the lower with their text. Its function is to determine, as nearly as may be, the precise form and language of a book as originally written down by its author; a task, the difficulty of which varies greatly in different cases, according to the age of the book and the extent and character of the evidence available. It is important, however, to recognise from the first that the problem is essentially the same, whether we are dealing with sacred or secular literature, although the difficulty of solving it, and likewise the issues depending on it, are very different. It is important, if for no other reason, because it is only in this way that we can meet the hostile critics of the New Testament with arguments, the force of which they admit. If we assume from the first the supernatural character of these books, and maintain that this affects the manner in which their text has come down to us, we can never convince those who start with a denial of that supernatural character. We treat them at first like any other books, in order to show at last that they are above and beyond all other books. It would be a lack of faith to doubt the issue of such an inquiry, and the history of New Testament criticism during the last two generations shows that doubt would be unfounded. The application of scientific criticism to the books of the New Testament, by laymen as well as by clerics, by classical scholars as well as by divines, has resulted in establishing them on a foundation more unassailable than ever.

But why, it may be asked, is criticism necessary in order to ascertain the precise text of the New Testament? The answer is simple. The necessity arises solely from the conditions under which books were written and circulated in ancient days. It is only since the invention of printing that there has been any possibility of guaranteeing that all copies of a book should be identical; and out of the eighteen hundred or eighteen hundred and fifty years which separate us from the time at which these books were written, only four hundred and fifty are covered by the existence of printing. Before printing was invented, every copy of a book must be separately written by hand; and, as those who have ever done much copying will know, by no possibility can the human hand and eye be kept from making mistakes. Mistakes, if not recognised, are perpetuated by later scribes; if recognised, they will often be wrongly corrected; and so the circle of error goes on widening from generation to generation. Of all the many thousand manuscript copies of the Bible in existence it may safely be asserted that no two are quite alike, and that none is wholly free from error.

The function of textual criticism, then, is the removal of these errors. The basis of its procedure lies in the comparison of all the available authorities. We must ascertain what copies of the book in question are in existence, and which of them come nearest in date to the lifetime of the original author. We must also make up our mind, by the application of the ordinary and common-sense canons of textual science, as to the comparative merits of the several authorities. Many errors are manifest; and a copy which has evidently been carelessly made will carry less weight in cases of doubt than one which has been transcribed with care. Often one of two rival readings is manifestly derived from the other; and a manuscript which is found to be addicted to such derivative readings will carry less weight than one which is free from this charge. By these and similar methods, all based upon common sense, but which would take too long to describe here, it is possible to gauge the character of manuscripts, to divide them into groups or classes, and to know what manuscripts or what class of manuscripts most deserve our confidence in cases of doubt.

Let us see, then, what resources are at our disposal for ascertaining the true text of the books of the New Testament. We do not possess, for example, the very copy of the Epistle which St. Paul sent to the Galatians, subscribed with large characters in his own hand, nor that which St. John wrote to the well-beloved Gaius with pen and ink; but we have many and ancient copies of them in their original language, and still more copies of translations of them into other tongues. The number of manuscript copies of the whole or parts of the New Testament exceeds immeasurably that which we have of any other work of ancient literature, and the earliest of them come nearer to the date at which the books were originally written. For most ancient Greek and Latin books the manuscript authorities must be counted by units or tens, very rarely by hundreds, while for the New Testament they must be reckoned by thousands; and if we find that, out of all these thousands, comparatively few reach the highest standard of trustworthiness, we must remember that in the case of most secular literature, for Æschylus, for Sophocles, for Plato, for Demosthenes, for Livy, for Tacitus, we are mainly dependent on one or at most two copies, the value of which far transcends that of all their companions.

The authorities for the text of the New Testament are of three kinds: first, manuscripts, or copies of it, or of parts of it, in the original Greek; secondly, ancient versions, or translations of it into other languages—Syriac, Latin, Coptic, and so on—which show us what form the Scriptures had when they were translated into those tongues; thirdly, quotations in ancient writers, which show us what sort of manuscripts the early Fathers of the Church used in different parts of the Christian world. It is only with the first of these classes, with the manuscripts in the original Greek, that I have to deal in this lecture. The versions will be treated by another hand in the next lecture of this course; while both I and my successor will have to refer to the evidence which the patristic quotations throw upon the character and history of the authorities with which we deal.

Of manuscripts containing the New Testament in Greek, or some part of it, more than three thousand are now known; and the question at once arises, how are we to choose among so great a crowd of witnesses? The first step naturally is to ask, how near do any of these manuscripts take us to the date of the original autographs? Now, setting aside a few small scraps, which will be mentioned again later, the earliest manuscripts of the New Testament are two, the Codex Vaticanus and the Codex Sinaiticus, which may be assigned, on fairly satisfactory grounds, to the fourth century. There is consequently an interval of about three hundred, or at least two hundred and fifty, years between the composition of the books of the New Testament and the earliest extant copies of them. Is there any explanation of this interval? Is there anything abnormal about it—anything which may be regarded as a ground of suspicion against the trustworthiness of the sacred Scriptures? Or, if not, at any rate what effect has this interval had on the state in which the Scriptures have come down to us? These are questions which suggest themselves, and to which an answer must be given.

In the first place, then, there is nothing abnormal in this state of things. The same state of things exists, in even greater measure, with regard to practically all the works of classical literature which have come down to us. With the exception of a few manuscripts on papyrus which have come to light of recent years, there are no classical manuscripts of earlier date than those of the New Testament, and that although the originals were composed several centuries before the Gospels and Epistles. There is nothing in this circumstance to cast doubt upon our sacred books; it is merely the result of the conditions under which books were produced before the fourth century of our era. To understand the problems of textual criticism, especially in the New Testament, it is necessary to bear in mind the conditions under which books were written and circulated in those far-off days.

During the first century of the Christian era, and for a considerable period both before and afterwards, the material upon which books were written, in all the countries in which the various parts of the New Testament were composed and copied, was papyrus. This material, made out of the pith of the papyrus plant, which at that time grew plentifully in Egypt, whence it was exported for use in other lands, was a somewhat delicate fabric, not at all calculated to resist the wear and tear of time. Originally perhaps about as strong as modern paper, it has become, in the specimens of it which still survive, so brittle that it cannot be handled without serious risk of damage, and would speedily crumble to pieces in the ordinary course of use as a book. Consequently it is only under exceptional circumstances that it has survived at all. In any ordinary climate, damp and decay have inevitably destroyed it; and the only place in which it has survived is in parts of Egypt above the Delta. There the soil and climate are so dry that even this fragile material, once buried in the ground, has continued to exist, becoming more brittle, it is true, and liable to mutilation in various ways, but still without losing legibility; and hence, from the tombs and rubbish heaps of buried Egyptian cities, have been disinterred the precious fragments of Greek literature, and the great mass of Greek business documents, which have rewarded explorers during the past century, and especially during the last fifteen years. But with these exceptions, all books written during the period when papyrus was the material in use have perished utterly, and the literature which they enshrined is known to us only in copies made at a later date, when papyrus had been superseded by a more durable fabric.

For more than two hundred years, consequently, the New Testament Scriptures circulated mainly, if not wholly, in this perishable material, and from this period only the scantiest remains have come down to us. A few scraps which can be assigned to the third century after Christ alone survive out of all the copies which may have once circulated in Egypt, while outside that country nothing at all is left. Had the Christian books been ordinary products of the literature of the day, and subject only to the same conditions as Æschylus and Sophocles, Herodotus and Thucydides, we still could not be surprised at the disappearance of all copies from this early period: for these authors have fared no better than St. Luke or St. Paul. But when we consider the position of Christians under the pagan Empire, there is still less room for wonder. The Christians were mainly a poor folk, not much given to reading or writing, and without free command of the ordinary means of book-production. In Alexandria, where conditions were more favourable, and in the Delta generally, the dampness of the soil is fatal to the survival of papyrus, so that all copies written in that part of the country have perished. Further, the Christians were liable to persecution, and the records of the persecutions show that their sacred books were often a principal object of search and destruction on the part of their persecutors. The copies possessed by the churches, which would be most likely to be carefully and correctly written, would also be the most likely to perish in this way. In many instances, we can hardly doubt, the tradition of the sacred text would be preserved only in the private copies made by individuals for their personal use; and these, as we can see from the example of similar copies of classical authors which have actually come down to us, would often be full of verbal and even substantial inaccuracies. Opportunities of rectifying errors by comparison with accurate copies at a distance or in other countries would be few, and hence divergences would increase and local types of text be formed. Moreover, in the early days, when the speedy coming of the Lord was expected, precise verbal accuracy was of less importance than the substance of the sacred record, and we cannot wonder if scribes felt at liberty to alter the wording of the narrative, or to insert incidents of our Lord's life which they believed to be authentic and valuable.

Another characteristic of ancient books must be mentioned, which had some effect on the textual history of the New Testament. During nearly the whole of the period in which papyrus was the predominant book-material, books were not written in pages, as they now are, but on continuous rolls. This fact has long been known from the statements of contemporary writers, but it is only of late years that specimens of such rolls have come to light in considerable numbers. We now possess papyrus rolls containing literary works, ranging from the third century before Christ to the third century after Christ, or to the seventh century if we include rolls containing non-literary documents; and consequently we know sufficiently well the general appearance of books at the time when the New Testament was written. Now these rolls seldom exceed a length of thirty feet; indeed they are generally shorter, and we must take it as certain that they were never appreciably longer. This is a length which, with medium-sized writing, will about suffice for one of the longer books of the New Testament,—one of the Gospels or the Acts; but it would certainly not hold more than one. Consequently we must regard the New Testament as circulating, not in complete volumes such as we now have, but in a number of separate rolls; and we must not suppose that every Christian had a complete set of them. Some would have one Gospel, some another; some books would be popular in one country, some in another; so that the fact that an early Christian writer quotes some books and not others affords no presumption that the latter did not exist or were not recognised as authoritative in his time. Also it must be remembered that the text was not divided into numbered chapters and verses. Divisions between sentences might be marked, though even this is not always the case; but that is all the aid which we find given to the reader of an ancient book, and it must have been far from easy to identify references. Hence we need not be surprised if early writers quote inexactly and from memory.

It is during the third century that we find a change coming over the methods of book-production. In the place of rolls, we begin to find rudimentary books. The material is still generally papyrus, but it is cut into pages, which are fastened together by strings passing through their left-hand margins, in imitation of the sets of wax tablets which were then (and previously) in use as note-books. To books of this kind—our modern book-form—the name of *codex* was given. At first they were used for note-books, or for inferior copies of works of literature, the roll form still holding its own for the better kind of copies. But the Christian writers, we may be sure, had often to make use of the inferior and cheaper forms of reproduction; and such evidence as has yet come to light tends to show that it was among the Christians especially that the codex form was first used to any great extent. The earliest extant examples of it nearly all contain Christian writings, while contemporary copies of pagan literature are still almost all in roll form. In the few leaves of these codices which remain to us from the third century—small and roughly-written for the most part, with little of the workmanship of the trained scribe—we may see the relics of the volumes which the earliest Christians used, easy to carry on the person, to pass from hand to hand, and easy also to conceal in days of persecution. But as roughly written books are seldom accurately copied, we must not be surprised if errors in detail crept largely into a literature which circulated so much in private and half-hidden ways.

During the third century, no doubt, the external conditions of Christianity were improving. Its congregations were larger and more important; toleration was more general; and it could hold its services and multiply its books with little interference from the populace or the civil power. But these improved conditions were liable to sharp breaches of continuity; and when persecution came, as under Decius in the middle of the third century and under Diocletian at the beginning of the fourth, it came with great severity. We know also, from the records of these persecutions, that a special point was made of the destruction of the sacred books, so that the surrender of them became an act specially marked among Christian congregations, into which inquiries were held, and for which punishments were inflicted, when the storm of persecution had gone by. On the whole, then, we must not look for any great amendment in the chances of survival for Christian manuscripts until the fourth century was well advanced in its course.

We reach here a critical point in the history, not only of Christian literature, but of Christianity itself. In 312 or 313 complete religious toleration throughout the Empire was proclaimed by Constantine; in 325 the Council of Nicaea was held; in 330 the new capital, Constantinople, was inaugurated with Christian ceremonial, and furnished by the emperor with Christian churches. There was no longer any obstacle to the free circulation of Christian literature; and at the same period a new departure of the greatest importance was made in book-production. This was the supersession of papyrus by vellum as the principal material upon which books were written. Of course the change was not made suddenly at a given moment. Vellum had long been used for note-books and inferior purposes, and during the third century it had been coming into use as a vehicle of literature. A few—very few—specimens have been found in Egypt which may be assigned to the second and third centuries; but outside Egypt, the special home of the papyrus, the change seems to have gone further. In the records of the search for books during the persecution of Diocletian in Africa, vellum codices and rolls (presumably of papyrus) are both mentioned, the former oftenest, so that we may conclude that the use of the new material was fairly well established by that time; but it was only in the fourth century that its supremacy was finally assured. Papyrus continued to be used, and books written upon it are extant as late as the seventh century, while in Egypt it remained in use still later, after the Arab conquest had practically closed the door to its export to the Christian world outside; but from the fourth century onwards vellum is the material regularly in use for the best copies of all works of literature.

This victory, which is marked for us by the fact that the copies of the Scriptures which Constantine ordered for the churches of his new capital were written upon vellum, is of fundamental importance in the history of textual criticism. In the first place, it now became possible to include all the books of the New Testament, or even of the whole Bible, in a single volume, a possibility which promoted the consideration, and so ultimately the determination, of the limits of the Canon. Secondly, the new material was infinitely more durable than papyrus, so much so that several volumes have lasted, often with little damage, from that day to this, and that not only, like papyrus, in the special climate of Egypt. It is in fact from the fourth century that the earliest extant manuscripts of the Greek Bible (small scraps excepted) have come down to us; and consequently it is from this point that we begin to gather in the materials of textual criticism.

In this manner the papyrus period may be characterised as the period in which the textual problems came into being, which we have to try to solve with the help of the evidence afforded by the later periods. This evidence can only be briefly summarised, its extent is so great. From the fourth century we have two great manuscripts, the Codex Vaticanus and the Codex Sinaiticus, the latter perfect, so far as the New Testament is concerned, the former wanting the Pastoral Epistles and the Apocalypse. It has been supposed by some that these are actually two of the fifty volumes prepared at the emperor's command by Eusebius of Caesarea for the churches of Constantinople; but for this identification there is no substantial evidence. They may have been written at Caesarea, but perhaps more probably in Egypt. To the fifth century probably belong two more great manuscripts, the Codex Alexandrinus and the Codex Ephraemi—the latter a mutilated palimpsest—and about twelve small fragments. To the sixth century are assigned the Codex Bezae of the Gospels and Acts, a manuscript in both Greek and Latin, of most remarkable character and great importance; the Codex Claromontanus, a Graeco-Latin MS. of

St. Paul's Epistles, and about thirty small fragments. The seventh, eighth, and ninth centuries add considerably to the totals of our manuscript authorities, though their individual importance diminishes as we pass further from the date of composition of the books contained in them.

So far, all our manuscripts are written in what is known as *uncial* writing; that is, in capital letters, each formed separately. Of such manuscripts, 129 are now reckoned in our lists, of which 47 contain some substantial portion of the New Testament, the rest being mere fragments. In the ninth century, however, a new kind of writing came into use, known as *minuscule*. This was a modification for literary purposes of the common writing of the day, and being far less cumbrous and inconvenient than the large and heavy uncial writing then in use, it rapidly superseded it as the main vehicle for literature. Beginning in the ninth century, and gaining a decisive victory in the tenth, from that point onwards it held its own, with modifications only in detail, until handwriting was superseded by print at the end of the fifteenth century. The greater ease of book-production brought about by the invention of the minuscule style led to a great increase of books, and especially of copies of the Scriptures; so that of minuscule copies of the New Testament, or of considerable portions of it, no less than three thousand are already reckoned in our lists.

Such being the mass of material, in manuscripts alone, with which the textual critic has to deal, it remains to ask what use has been, or can be, made of it. Let me begin by suggesting another question. How many of these manuscripts, do you suppose, were consulted in the preparation of the printed text which we find in our common Greek Testaments, and from which our Authorised Version was made? Perhaps between twenty and thirty in all; and these selected neither for age nor excellence, but for the most part because they were the manuscripts which happened to be at the editor's disposal. The first printed edition of the Greek New Testament, that of Erasmus in 1516, was based on five MSS., and mainly upon three only—one for the Gospels, one for the Acts and Epistles, and one for the Apocalypse, all comparatively late minuscule copies. A comparison of this text with that of the Complutensian edition and with fifteen MSS., mostly minuscule copies at Paris, produced the edition of Stephanus in 1550; and Stephanus' text, with very slight modifications, is our Received Text to the present day. Only one uncial manuscript, the Codex Bezae, appears to have been taken into consideration at all, and that but slightly. All the other ancient authorities were either unknown or unexamined.

Consider then in what a different position we stand to-day. Since the date of the establishment of the Received Text, and since the publication of the Authorised Version in 1611, scholars have been busy in the collection of evidence from all quarters, from manuscripts, from ancient versions, and from quotations in the early Fathers. The process may be said to begin with the great poly-glott Bible of Bishop Brian Walton, of which the New Testament was published in 1657; and it is not finished yet. Within the last few months two valuable uncial manuscripts have come to light, one a sixth century fragment of St. Matthew, written in letters of gold upon purple vellum, the other a nearly complete copy of the Gospels of the ninth century; while the harvest gleaned from Versions and the Fathers increases day by day. It is not necessary to describe the accumulation of evidence in detail, but a few salient points may be indicated. It is a process which falls into two parts, the first being the collection of evidence, and the second its classification and use. In the department of collection, the model for all future workers was set by Dr. John Mill, whose edition, the fruit of thirty years' labour, was published in 1707. Other scholars followed in his tracks, and for the next 150 years it was the collection of evidence which was the principal care of textual scholars. Not until the nineteenth century was well advanced did any critic set his hand to using the accumulated material for a revision of the Received Text. In this department of criticism the pioneer was the German scholar, Karl Lachmann, who applied to the text of the New Testament the principles which he had learnt in the study of classical literature. Selecting from the mass of authorities then at his disposal those which seemed to him the oldest and the best, he constructed from them a revised Greek text of the New Testament, which was printed first in 1831, and again, with fuller annotation, in 1842-1850.

Lachmann was followed by a pair of scholars who have left a deep mark in the history of textual criticism, Tischendorf and Tregelles. Tischendorf had the good fortune to discover the great Codex Sinaiticus, as well as a large number of uncial fragments; but Tregelles was not behind him in labour or skill. Both were indefatigable collators of manuscripts; both applied their collations to the preparation of revised Greek texts. Both did much to demonstrate, and did indeed demonstrate conclusively, that the Received Text rested on a slender basis of inferior materials, and that, although the substance of the Scriptures was, no doubt, faithfully preserved in it, yet in details it was capable of much amendment. Their labours went far to establish the necessity for a revision of the Received Text, and therewith of the Authorised Version.

One step yet remained to take; a step of great importance. In dealing with manuscripts of classical literature, it is usual (now, indeed, universal) to try to divide them into groups, according to their relationships to each other. Some MSS. can be shown to be copied, directly or indirectly, from others; some to be descendants from a common original nearer to the author's autograph; some to represent a revision undertaken by a mediaeval editor; while of such groups or families some can be shown to be distinctly preferable to others, and consequently to deserve credence in cases which otherwise would be doubtful. So far, no one had succeeded in applying this system to the manuscripts of the New Testament. Tentative classifications had indeed been made by a few scholars, of whom the most distinguished was Griesbach, about the end of the 18th century; but their classifications had been rejected by their contemporaries, and even they themselves had not ventured to apply them to the actual restoration of the Biblical text.

This step was taken by the two great Cambridge

scholars, whose names are household words in the history of textual criticism, Bishop Westcott and Dr. Hort. A knowledge of their principles, and of the conclusions to which they came, is essential for the understanding of the textual criticism of to-day; for at the present time every scholar and critic of note takes off from the theory which they laid down. This theory can be outlined in a few words. An examination of the evidence which has been collected from Manuscripts, Versions, and Fathers shows that, in cases where differences exist, certain authorities are found habitually to agree with one another, and to be in opposition to certain other groups similarly formed. Thus groups can be distinguished, each having presumably some common ancestor, short of the original author's autograph; and we are then in a position to go further, to estimate the comparative value of each of these groups, and to try to locate their respective ancestors in space and time, that is, to determine where and when the types of text which they represent came into existence. It will be evident very shortly how this is done.

Westcott and Hort, following the lines laid down by Griesbach, but following them more elaborately, distinguished four classes or groups in the authorities for the text of the New Testament. First, there is the group to which the Received Text belongs ; a group to which, moreover, the vast majority of manuscripts belongs ; a group which has had the preponderance in the textual tradition at least since the 6th century. This group Westcott and Hort, for reasons which will appear shortly, call the *Syrian* group. Those who prefer a more colourless, and therefore less question-begging, name, may indicate it by the first letter of the Greek alphabet and call it the *Alpha*-group (α). Secondly, there is a group to which the earliest extant manuscripts belong, the Codex Vaticanus and the Codex Sinaiticus, supported by a few later uncials and minuscules, and by one, and to some extent two, of the ancient Egyptian versions. This group Westcott and Hort call the *Neutral* group, indicating thereby their belief in its superiority to its rivals ; our alternative name for it would be the *Beta*-group (β). The third group is only, so to speak, a sub-species of the last named, found when there is a difference among the authorities of that group. Such differences Westcott and Hort believed to be due to slight verbal alterations, made probably to suit the taste of that great centre of literary criticism, Alexandria ; consequently they call it *Alexandrian*. The more cautious name for it is the *Gamma*-group (γ). Finally there is a considerable quantity of authorities, generally of very early date, marked by strong divergences, of addition, of subtraction, and of verbal variation, from all the other groups. They also differ considerably among themselves, and it is difficult to suppose that they can trace their origin to a common ancestor, but they resemble one another sufficiently in the character of their divergences to justify their being grouped together. The most notable manuscript belonging to this group is the Graeco-Latin Codex Bezae, with which are allied some other bilingual manuscripts; but this type of text is better represented by some of the oldest versions, notably the Old Latin and the Old Syriac Versions. The marked appearance of Latin authorities in this group led Westcott and Hort to call it the *Western* group; but the name is misleading, and consequently here, even more than elsewhere, a non-committal name is preferable, and it may be called the *Delta*-group (δ).

Now, so far as the greater part of the words of the New Testament are concerned, there are no differences between the authorities which need be taken into account; and so far as the main events and doctrines contained in them are concerned, it may be said at once that here too there are no differences, though in some important passages there are divergences in the exact wording. When, however, differences of reading do occur, and we find that the authorities are divided into the four groups which have just been enumerated, on what principles can we decide between them? To some extent a decision can be made upon the intrinsic merits of the several readings. Thus in some cases one reading has obviously been developed out of the other; in others it is possible to suppose that a false reading has been imported into a passage from another passage in which the context is similar—a form of error peculiarly likely to happen in the Synoptic Gospels, though the extent to which an editor will admit it must depend upon his theory as to the origin and composition of the synoptic books. But such decisions rest largely on the prepossessions and personal equation of the critic, and we want a more objective criterion. Such a criterion would be provided if we could trace the history of the various groups of authorities, and so learn which of them has the oldest and most trustworthy ancestors. The essential part of the theory of Westcott and Hort lies in their provision of this criterion.

It is in the evidence of the early Fathers that the solution of the problem is to be found. By an examination of the quotations from the Scriptures which occur in their writings it is possible to see what sort of manuscripts they used, and to which of our four groups (if to any) these manuscripts belonged; and then we can take a step further and see to what date and to what country our groups can severally be assigned. Now the corner-stone of Westcott and Hort's theory lies in the observation that no characteristic reading of the α-group is found in any of the Fathers before the period of Chrysostom—that is, before the latter part of the 4th century. The presumption consequently is that this type of text is of relatively late date, due either to a revision accomplished at some particular time, or, perhaps more probably, to the result of a revising process continued over a period of time. This conclusion is supported by the fact that readings of this type often appear, on examination, to be the result of such modifications of readings occurring in the other groups as might naturally be made in the interests of smoother language or the removal of apparent difficulties. It follows that when a reading is supported solely by authorities belonging to this family (which consists, as above stated, mainly of the later uncials and the great mass of the minuscules), there is a strong presumption that it is not the original text, but the result of a relatively late revision. It is the removal of such readings which causes the greater part of the differences in the text adopted by the Revisers of our Bible from that which underlies the Authorised Version.

Upon this point, namely, the secondary character, as it may be called, of the α-text, critics are now generally agreed; the advocates of the old Received Text are now few and far between. But when we come to the remaining families, and have to make a choice between them, it is less easy to arrive at a decision. The third family (what we have called the γ-group) may indeed be left out of the question for the present, because it consists mainly of merely verbal modifications of the second; but between the second and the fourth (the β and δ-groups) there is much need for a decision, while the grounds for the decision are far from clear. Neither can be ruled out by the evidence of the Fathers as certainly later than the other. Both have early and good attestation. On the one hand we have the β-text supported by the oldest Greek manuscript, the Codex Vaticanus, commonly recognised by critics, even before and apart from this particular stage of the controversy, as not only the oldest but also the most trustworthy single witness to the New Testament: by the Codex Sinaiticus, next to the Vaticanus in age, and akin to it in character, yet also differing so much that their common ancestor must be removed by several generations from them, and hence cannot be placed far below the date of the original autographs; by some fragments of early manuscripts (notably those known as T Z R Ξ); by the late but remarkable codex L of the Gospels, and a few of the minuscules, which are evidently descended from ancestors of the same type; and by one of the two main Coptic versions of the New Testament (the Bohairic), with some support from the other (the Sahidic); while it also appears that the manuscripts used by Jerome in preparing the Vulgate Latin version belonged to this group. Besides Jerome, who thus showed his preference (the preference of a professed textual scholar) for this type of text, the great Greek textual critic, Origen, also mainly used manuscripts of this type, and occasionally Clement of Alexandria. From all these authorities it is possible to form a coherent text of the New Testament with great claims on our acceptance, backed as it is by ancient and trustworthy witnesses, some of them being certainly, and others very possibly, associated with Egypt, and especially with the great literary centre of that country, Alexandria.

On the other hand we have in the δ-group a large quantity of readings, markedly divergent from all the other groups, not uniformly or consistently found in any one set of authorities, but scattered unevenly among many authorities in many parts of the world. In other words, there are several manuscripts and versions which frequently have readings of this strongly marked class, but they will seldom be found all united in the support of any one reading. Hence it is doubtful whether they can be referred to a single ancestor, rather than to a tendency to laxity in transcription manifested in different places; and it is misleading to speak of the δ-group as a single family in the same sense as the α and β-groups may be so described. Intrinsically, therefore, with their wide divergences and wavering attestation, readings of this type would not, as a rule, carry much weight. What gives them authority is the very early date of the witnesses which support them. So far as manuscripts, indeed, are concerned, they cannot rival the β-group. The principal manuscripts of this group are the Graeco-Latin Codex Bezae of the Gospels and Acts of the sixth century; the Graeco-Latin Codex Claromontanus of the Pauline Epistles of the same period; the Graeco-Latin Codex Laudianus of the Acts of the 7th century; four other late Graeco-Latin codices of the Pauline Epistles; with occasional support from the Codex Sinaiticus and other uncials, and several minuscules. These authorities in themselves would not suffice to establish any great age for this type of text, and the presence of a Latin version in so many of them would point to an origin in the West. But it is also supported by the oldest versions, the Old Latin and the Old Syriac, the origin of which probably goes back to the 2nd century, and predominantly by the Sahidic, which is probably the earliest Egyptian version, and may have been made in the third century. Of these remarkable versions more will be said in the next lecture of this course. But more notable still is the evidence of the Fathers. It is not too much to say that *all* the earliest writers who quote the New Testament sufficiently to enable us to discern what type of text they used must have used manuscripts of this character; and they are not confined to any single country. Justin Martyr, Tatian, Marcion, Irenaeus, in the second century, Clement of Alexandria and (to a less certain extent) Tertullian at the end of the second century and beginning of the third, Cyprian and sometimes even Origen in the third, the Syriac writers Aphraates and Ephraem and the African Tyconius in the fourth—all these show by their quotations that they used manuscripts akin in character to the Old Latin and Old Syriac versions, and their witness is spread over all parts of the Christian world—Syria, Egypt, Africa, Italy, and Gaul. Evidence so early and so wide-spread cannot be ignored, difficult though it may be to co-ordinate it.

This, then, is the textual problem which confronts scholars at the present day. Putting aside the claims of the α-text, our old Received Text, as being now superseded by almost the common consent of critics of all countries, we have on the one hand the β-text, comparatively homogeneous in character, early in attestation, but somewhat limited to the locality, or at least the sphere of influence, of Alexandria; on the other, the δ-text, supported by very early and widely distributed attestation, but far from homogeneous in character, so that it is often difficult to choose between two or more readings supported by authorities all of which belong to this class. How can we decide between them? or how can we account for the existence of this state of affairs?

As will be seen from the next lecture, there is much to be said in support of the δ-text, and some of the best authorities on the subject are prepared to go far in the advocacy of its claims,—further than I myself should be prepared to go. The problem is still unsolved, and various methods may rightly be tried in order to solve it. It may be suggested, however, that the key lies in the history of the circulation of the Scriptures during the first two centuries of their existence, of which some sketch was given at the beginning of this lecture. The earliest Christians neither felt the need, nor had they the means, of securing precise accuracy in the transmission of the documents of their faith. At first they were not even sacred books at all. The Gospels were simply narratives written by or under the influence of apostles, four of which stood out slightly or not at all among a number of others; the Epistles were merely the letters of St. Paul or St. Peter, St. John or St. James or St. Jude, written to various churches for the purpose of instruction or exhortation. There was no obvious reason why additions, believed to be authentic, should not be made to the narrative of our Lord's life, nor why precise verbal accuracy should be insisted on in transcription. The second coming of the Lord was looked for shortly; it was the substance of the message that mattered, not its exact words.

Hence it is not surprising if variations crept into the record to a considerable extent, even in the earliest times; and when once in, it was not easy to expel them. Free circulation and comparison of manuscripts was difficult in the early days, when Christians were few and widely scattered, and also later, when repression was apt to follow on too great activity. Public copying and circulation of the sacred books was always precarious, and in times of persecution the books were a special object of search and destruction. Hence there was no such possibility of the establishment of a standard text, and the removal of all variations therefrom, as existed at a later period for the Jewish scriptures, or to some extent for the classical writers; and even in these, as we know, errors crept in plentifully during the manuscript period. For the first two centuries of the existence of the Christian books, the course of their textual tradition runs through irregular channels, through private, uncorrected, copies, transcribed often by unskilled hands in villages of Egypt or Syria or Asia, not through an ordered sequence of official copies, transcribed in great libraries by trained scribes and under the eye of an experienced corrector.

Only in one place can we see that a more favourable state of things may have existed. Alexandria was not only the headquarters of trained scholarship in the Greek world; it was also the centre of the Jewish colony in Egypt and of Jewish learning in the world at large. There the Septuagint version of the Old Testament had been prepared; and there, we may be fairly certain, was the first Christian church in Egypt founded. By the end of the second century we find a strong Christian community established there, with a flourishing Catechetical School, of which Clement and Origen were successive heads. There, if anywhere, we might expect a pure text of the Christian books to be sought for and preserved; and while irregularity and indifference to precise accuracy are easily explicable in Syria and Asia Minor and Africa, we may fairly hope for better things in Egypt, and especially in such a centre of literary scholarship as Alexandria.

These *a priori* considerations harmonise well with the facts as we find them, and as they have been described above. The β-text, which Westcott and Hort call the neutral text, has evident associations, as we have seen, with Egypt, and even with the school of Origen; while the δ-text or texts may represent the condition of the Scripture text in the rest of the Christian world. Consequently it seems not unreasonable to give one's confidence to the former, with its internal appearance of accuracy and its external associations with traditions of good scholarship, rather than to its irregular and eccentric competitor, in spite of the wide distribution of texts of the latter character. At the same time it is not fair to represent the issue as finally closed. On the contrary, there is an increasing tendency among many scholars, whose labours and knowledge entitle them to all respect, to look with favour on readings attested by authorities of the δ-text, especially when they are supported by witnesses from both the main groups of their family, the Latin and the Syriac. To some extent one may be prepared to go with them, and at least to give their arguments in each case a respectful hearing; for as between these two ancient types of text it is not likely that the Alexandrian tradition is always right and its competitor always wrong. The very ancient variants found in the various authorities of the δ-type must always be looked upon with interest. Right or wrong, they circulated largely in the Christian Church of the second century, and were regarded as authentic by great Fathers of the Church, such as Justin and Irenaeus and Cyprian; and sometimes they may embody authentic traditions, even though they be no original part of the books in which we now find them.

In the space of this lecture, it has not been possible to give concrete examples of various readings characteristic of the several textual families which have been described. But it may be possible, in conclusion, to give some idea of them, and of the issues which are involved in textual criticism, by a reference to certain texts and translations easily accessible and known to many. Our familiar Authorised Version, and the Greek texts printed in the ordinary Greek Testaments, represent the α-text or Received Text, and that not in its best form, being derived, as we saw, from a comparatively small number of late and casually chosen manuscripts. The β-text is embodied most thoroughly in the Greek Testament of Westcott and Hort, who are its special champions; but in a modified form it underlies our Revised Version. Bishop Ellicott, the venerable President of the New Testament Committee, has lately emphasised the fact that the Revisers did not wholly surrender themselves to the guidance of Bishop Westcott and Dr. Hort;[1] but their text is in the main due to the adoption of a similar view as to the comparative merits of the principal manuscripts, and on the whole it is not unfair to say that it represents the kind of text which will be arrived at from an acceptance of the principles advocated in this lecture. If we are to go further, and recognise to any great extent the authority of the δ-text, we must be prepared for much more marked divergences from the traditional text; for the addition of one or two sayings of our Lord which have not hitherto found a place in our Bibles; for the omission of several passages in the later chapters of St. Luke (as noted in the margin of the Revised Version); and for considerable alterations in detail, especially in the narrative portions of the Acts of the Apostles.

One thing alone we need not fear; and that is that any modifications of text upon manuscript authority will affect the fundamental doctrines of our faith. In one form as in the other, the Scriptures testify with equal clearness of Christ, and the foundations of Christianity stand firm. It is with details, not with essentials, that we have to deal; and in the determination of them we can surely let ourselves be guided by the use of the best faculties

[1] *The Revised Version of Holy Scripture*, by C. J. Ellicott, D.D., Bishop of Gloucester, pp. 56-63 (S.P.C.K., 1901).

of intellect and judgment which God has given us. If, as critical science assuredly leads us to believe, the Revised Version contains a nearer approximation to the words originally spoken by Christ and written down by apostle or evangelist, then surely its claim on our acceptance overpowers even that of our venerable and beautiful Authorised Version. At least one may plead that they should be used side by side, the more accurate text being used to check and verify and explain the more familiar, until both alike are familiar and we have come to see how great is the preponderance of clearness and authenticity on the part of that text, which, though seeming new to us, yet rests upon the oldest and most trustworthy authorities. *Fortis est veritas et praevalebit.*

The Ancient Versions of the New Testament.

THE New Testament is a collection of books and letters written originally in Greek, which it seemed good to the Christian Church to place side by side with the Sacred Books that the Church had inherited from the Jews. A generation after the crucifixion of our Lord the Church had already become to a great extent a Greek-speaking community, and the process was completed by the great catastrophe of the Jewish War. The Church of Jerusalem practically ceased to exist, and the Aramaic-speaking Christianity of Palestine perished with it. It is not too much to say that for more than two generations after the destruction of Jerusalem by Titus the Christian Churches were communities of people who spoke Greek and very little else.

This is the dark age of Christianity. At the

close of the period, that is to say about the middle of the second century of our era, the Catholic Church emerges, undeveloped indeed, but still recognisably the same as the Church of succeeding ages in its organisation, its theology, and its sacred books. The New Testament of the latter half of the second century is in its main features—the Four Gospels, the Acts, the Epistles of Saint Paul—identical with the New Testament which we receive to-day.

It was about this time, during the latter half of the second century, that Christian communities sprang up in which Greek was a foreign tongue. For a long time, we do not know how long, the Church in Rome was a Greek-speaking body. The early Bishops of Rome had Greek names. The letter of S. Clement of Rome, written about the end of the first century to the Christians of Corinth, is in Greek. Justin Martyr, who lived at Rome about the middle of the second century, wrote in Greek; so also did his contemporary Hermas, brother of Pope Pius I. But the Christians of Lyons in Gaul, and still more certainly the Christians of Carthage, the capital of the Roman Province of Africa, were folk to whom Latin was the language of daily life. Such communities would not long be content to have their sacred books left in a foreign tongue, and that the tongue of wandering traders and slaves. The provincial Latin might be rude and mixed with Greek and Barbarian idioms, but it was in theory and in the minds of the provincials themselves the Imperial tongue, in no way unsuitable for the deepest thought and the most solemn occasions. The course was clear, in Carthage certainly, in southern Gaul probably, for a Latin Version of the Bible.

The exact date of the first Latin Version of the Bible, or indeed of any part of the Bible, is uncertain. It is a remarkable fact that the Latin Churches do not seem to have retained any memory of this great event in their history. We have no legend, no tradition to go upon, and we are reduced to building up a theory from scattered indications. Under these circumstances it is better to begin at the end, at a point where we have the light of contemporary history. If we know but little about the earliest translations of the New Testament into Latin, we do know the history of the Revised Version which supplanted them, the Version I mean which is familiar to us under the name of the Vulgate.

In the last quarter of the 4th century the need of some measure of uniformity began to make itself felt, and Pope Damasus commissioned S.

Jerome, the most learned scholar in western Christendom, to prepare a Revised Latin Version. In accordance with this plan S. Jerome published his text of the Gospels in 383 A.D., the rest of the New Testament appearing some years afterwards. The version was at once accepted by S. Augustine, and gradually made its way into general favour. Substantially in its original form the Vulgate has been used by the Western Church for over 1200 years, and it was from the Vulgate that all the early English translations of the Bible were made from the days of the Heptarchy to Wycliffe.

The texts which S. Jerome's Revision were designed to supersede are known to modern scholars under the general name of the Old Latin Versions. The MSS. which preserve these pre-Vulgate texts differ very greatly from one another, so much so that S. Jerome declared that in his day almost every copy had a distinct type of text. But the general opinion of scholars now is that there were not more than one, or at the most two, independent translations from the Greek. The differences seem to have arisen rather from revisions of an already existing translation than from an entirely fresh start.

The oldest form of the Latin version, of which enough has survived for us to get a clear idea of its style and character, is that used by S. Cyprian, Bishop of Carthage from 248-258 A.D., *i.e.* about 130 years before S. Jerome's version. S. Cyprian was a most diligent and accurate quoter, and his works are well preserved in many ancient MSS. By comparing his quotations with our MSS. of the N.T. in Latin we find that his version survives in a fragmentary copy of S. Mark and S. Matthew now at Turin, called *Codex Bobiensis* (*k*), and in the fragments of the Apocalypse and of the Acts contained in a Palimpsest at Paris, called *Codex Floriacensis* (*h*). Besides these two we may mention a *Codex Palatinus* (*e*) at Vienna, which has on the whole a Cyprianic text, though it is not free from mixture with later and more commonplace elements. For the Apocalypse we also have the Commentary of the late African Primasius.

The identification of the African text is too important a fact to be slurred over. As far as our fragments carry us, that is to say, for the last half of S. Mark, the first half of S. Matthew, several pages of the Acts, and practically the whole of the Apocalypse, we have the text of the New Testament as read in the capital of Roman Africa in the year 250 A.D. It is true that our MSS. contain some faults, but they are faults of transcription such as can for the most part be corrected; they do not greatly hinder us in the work of reconstructing the Greek text of which these fragments are a translation.

That is after all our chief task—*reconstructing the Greek text from which the Latin is a translation.* The ultimate use of a version of the N.T. to the textual critic is that it tells him what the text of the original Greek was like at the time of the translation. And the value of this reconstructed Greek to us depends very greatly upon the age to which we can actually trace it back. If we are to feel any confidence that this or that phrase or 'various reading' is the actual word of the original writer, I feel sure it must be because we can really trace back the phrase in question to the earliest times, not because it happens to have commended itself to some critic of the ancient or modern world.

To come back to S. Cyprian. The recension used by him is the oldest that survives in our MSS., but we are able to carry the history of the Bible in Latin somewhat further. The Cyprianic text was itself not a primitive translation but a revision, and traces of a somewhat different type of text survive in the quotations of one of S. Cyprian's fellow-bishops,[1] Nemesianus of Thubunae on the borders of Numidia. A generation before S. Cyprian

[1] See C. H. Turner in *Jour. of Theol. Studies*, ii. 602-607.

we have the numerous Biblical quotations and allusions in Tertullian's works, but these must be used with great caution. Tertullian knew Greek, and there are indications that he often made his quotations by direct translation from his Greek MS. This much at least is clear, that at Carthage in the first half of the 3rd century some books of the Old Testament were revised from Greek sources. Tertullian quotes Daniel from the LXX. version; S. Cyprian, and his contemporary, the author of the *Computus de Pascha* (A.D. 243), use Theodotion's version, though in S. Cyprian's case there is a large admixture of LXX. readings. On the other hand, Tertullian's quotations from Ezekiel contain many readings derived from Theodotion, a curious circumstance which has a parallel in some of the quotations of Clement of Alexandria a little earlier. But S. Cyprian's quotations from Ezekiel present what we are accustomed to consider a pure LXX. text.

Confusing as these details are in many respects, they show at least one thing—that the Latin Bible of 250 A.D. had a long and complicated history behind it. We need not therefore be surprised that the Scillitan martyrs, who suffered at Carthage in the year 180 A.D., had in their book-chest 'epistles of Paul, the just man,' and apparently a copy of the Gospels also. In the trial of these martyrs there is no hint that they were acquainted with Greek, so it naturally follows that their books were in Latin.

The history of the Latin translation of the Bible is even more obscure in the earlier stages of its development in Europe than in Africa. We first catch a glimpse of it in Gaul as early as A.D. 177, the date of the persecution of the Churches of Vienne and Lyons. An account of this persecution, written by the persecuted Churches to their brethren in Asia and Phrygia, is preserved in Eusebius.[1] This account is in Greek, but Canon Armitage Robinson has shown that the author of the letter was more familiar with a Latin Version of the N.T. than with the original Greek text, and this Latin Version was akin to the recensions used by Tertullian and S. Cyprian.[2]

A few years later appeared the great work of S. Irenaeus, Bishop of Lyons—the very place where we have seen reason to believe that a Latin version of the N.T. was current—but his confutation of the Gnostics was written in Greek, and it is very doubtful when the Latin translation of it was made. So far as materials for comparison survive, the renderings of Biblical quotations in the Latin trans-

---

[1] Eus. *H.E.*, v. 1 ff.

[2] See *The Passion of S. Perpetua*, by J. Armitage Robinson (1891), p. 97 ff.

lation of Irenaeus do not agree with those familiar to the writer of the Letter of the Churches of Vienne and Lyons.[1]

Thus S. Irenaeus contributes little to our knowledge, and after him the history of Christianity in Gaul is a blank for nearly a hundred and fifty years.

For the text of the N.T. as read in Italy about A.D. 250 we have the quotations of Novatian and the Roman correspondents of S. Cyprian. Then comes another blank period, which lasts till the middle of the next century, but from that time the evidence is continuous, and (it may be added) complicated. The 4th century was the age of mixture, the age when the Church unified its confession of faith and began to codify its ritual. The final result was a great measure of uniformity, but it was attained by much antecedent *confusion*—the pouring together of what had previously been separate. And so it comes to pass that when we approach our MSS., the oldest of which may be assigned to the 4th century or the beginning of the 5th, we find that very few of them represent

[1] The translator of Irenaeus (*Mass.* 279) renders ἔνδυμα γάμου in Matt. xxii. 12 by *indumentum nuptiarum*, but there is reason to believe that the author of the Letter of the Churches of Vienne and Lyons here read *uestimentum nuptiale* or *ueste nuptiali*, since he uses the phrase αἴσθησιν ἐνδύματος νυμφικοῦ (Robinson's *Perpetua*, p. 99).

a single type of text. Out of more than a dozen MSS. of the Gospels in Latin which may fairly be classed as pre-Vulgate, one, Cod. Bobiensis (*k*), as I have already said, gives the Cyprianic text with considerable fidelity; another, Cod. Palatinus (*e*), is predominantly Cyprianic; another, Cod. Vercellensis (*a*), gives in S. John the text as read by Lucifer of Cagliari. The rest represent mixed texts, of which we can only say that such texts were current in Italy and Gaul (and especially in N. Italy) during the 4th and 5th centuries. In many instances the MSS. differ in the underlying Greek from that represented by *k* and S. Cyprian; it is quite evident that we have to do with textual as well as literary revision. At the same time they all seem to come from a common stock; Novatian and his friends stand about half way between the Africans and the main body of the European MSS., and there are not wanting notable common readings and even common blunders which bind all or most of the Latins together.

To give a most familiar instance, none the less significant for being so familiar. S. Luke tells us that the shepherds heard the Angelic host singing "Glory to God in the highest, and on earth peace ἐν ἀνθρώποις εὐδοκία." At least this is what nearly all our Greek MSS. give us, and the Eastern versions agree. Thus the last words mean "Goodwill among men." But the Latin translator (in agreement with four of our Greek MSS. and these the oldest) read [ἐν] ἀνθρώποις εὐδοκίας, and so the Latin rendering of the half verse is *et in terra pax hominibus bonae uoluntatis*, *i.e.* "and on earth peace to men of good will." We need not now consider which of these two readings is right—εὐδοκία or εὐδοκίας—what is important for our present purpose is that the reading which is *not* supported by the Latin texts was by far the more common in Greek MSS. The fact of the agreement of all the Latins in the phrase *hominibus bonae uoluntatis*—"to men of good will"—is a proof that the many Latin texts are ultimately derived from a common primitive translation, and that fragments of this common primitive translation survive in our MSS. notwithstanding corrections and revisions.

But the Latin texts do not always agree together, and the primitive translation often survives only in a single branch. By far the largest proportion of ancient readings comes from the African side, from the Cyprianic text. It is in Roman Africa that the Greek element is least obtrusively present; it must have been in Roman Africa, of all the great centres of population, that Greek MSS. were least abundant. Consequently we often find that African texts give us what is only found elsewhere in some Oriental source, while the rest of our

Latin texts support the common reading. In such cases we are justified in assuming the African reading to have been that of the primitive Latin version, and that in our other Latin texts a supposed mistake has been corrected out by the aid of later Greek MSS. The dissimilarity between the African Bible and that of the Greeks was clearly perceived by S. Augustine at the end of the 4th century. But he went upon the theory that the Greek reading as known to him was nearly always right, and so he did less than justice to the faithfulness of his vernacular Bible.

Before leaving the Latin versions I am sure you will forgive me for saying a word or two upon the texts which were once current in our own country. S. Patrick, himself a native of Great Britain, started on his missionary journey to Ireland about A.D. 405, at a time when S. Jerome's revision, which we call the Vulgate, had not yet supplanted the Old Latin in Britain, or even in France, where S. Patrick had been trained. The N.T. therefore reached Ireland in an Old Latin, a pre-Vulgate, form. After the conversion of Ireland the heathen English took possession of the best part of what is now England and the Lowlands of Scotland, and with the downfall of British Christianity came the disappearance of the Old Latin texts. When the English in their turn were converted through the labours of S. Augustine of Canterbury and those who came after him, the material things of the Christian Church—paintings, glass, and also books—had in the first instance to be fetched from Italy, and coming as they did from the headquarters of Christendom, the copies of the Bible thus brought contained a very pure Vulgate text. By a singular and happy accident a copy of one of these foreign Bibles, made at Monkwearmouth or at Jarrow early in the 8th century, was brought to Italy in the year 715, and now rests in the Laurentian Library at Florence. The *Codex Amiatinus*, as it is called, is for modern scholars the leading MS. of the Vulgate; and it is interesting to remember that it was made in England for export to the Continent.

The Irish Church, after long hesitation, laid aside the usages which separated it from the rest of Christendom, and among other changes adopted the Vulgate in place of the Old Latin. The most distinctive date in a long process, which only ended with the conquest of Ireland by Henry II., was the adoption of the Roman tonsure by Adamnan, Abbot of Iona, a little before 700 A.D. The Vulgate text thenceforward current in Ireland was nevertheless mixed with readings derived from Old Latin sources, and a MS. of the 7th century is still preserved at Trinity College, Dublin, the text of which is almost wholly independent of the Vulgate. Of all the monuments of Christianity in these islands, a few gravestones excepted, this *Codex Usserianus* is the one least influenced by the coming of the English.

We turn now from the extreme West to the East, from one end of the Roman Empire to the other. The translation of the N.T. into Syriac took place about the same time as the translation of the N.T. into Latin, and it is almost as important an event in the history of the text. Syriac is a dialect of Aramaic, akin to the Aramaic of Palestine, the language of our Lord and His apostles. There is therefore a special interest in the renderings adopted by the Syriac translator, as many of the words used in his translation of the Gospels must have been identical with those originally spoken. The mere fact that the Syriac translation has *Messiah* for 'the Christ' and *Cephas* for 'Peter' is enough to show the connection between the Aramaic of the Euphrates Valley and the Aramaic of Palestine. At the same time it must not be supposed that the Syriac versions are anything but translations from the Greek, or that Syriac Christianity had any special historical link with the primitive Christianity of Palestine. The head-quarters of Syriac Christianity was Edessa, which until the year 216 A.D. was the capital of an independent principality east of the Euphrates and the Roman Empire. Christianity was planted there from the Greek city of Antioch, and not from Palestine: to use their own way of putting it, the bishops of Edessa traced their succession from Rome and not from Jerusalem.

Edessa, as I have just said, was an independent principality. The language there spoken was the language of a court; it was also the language of commerce all the way down the Euphrates Valley and in the adjoining provinces, a language with literary and social prestige. When therefore Christianity began to spread in Edessa in the latter half of the second century, the ground was ready for the work of translation. The ease and fluency of the earliest Christian literature in Syriac shows that Syriac was a literary language before the Syriac-speaking peoples came in contact with Christianity.

The point is really important, because other conditions prevailed elsewhere. Until the fourth century, or at the earliest the end of the third, the Christian Egyptians used Greek as their ecclesiastical language: in their country the language of literature and of the official world was Greek. Until the end of the fourth century the Christian Armenians used Syriac as their ecclesiastical language: in their country the language of literature was Syriac. But Latin in the West and Syriac in the East were literary languages before the coming of Christianity, and they were moreover the language of a ruling class. Accordingly into these languages, and these languages alone, the New Testament was translated in the second century.

The history of the N.T. in Syriac is in most respects similar to the history of the N.T. in Latin. We have an Old Syriac Version of unknown age, the MSS. of which differ considerably from one another, partly owing to irregular revision from later Greek MSS. The confusion and variety which ensued was finally brought to an end by the triumph of an authoritative revision, which is now known by the name of the *Peshitta*. The Peshitta has been ever since the fifth century the Vulgate of all branches of the Syriac-speaking Church; I have elsewhere given reasons for believing that it was published under the auspices of Rabbula, the friend and correspondent of Cyril of Alexandria and Bishop of Edessa from 411 to 435 A.D.[1] Rabbula's biographer tells us that on his appointment to his see "by the wisdom of God that was in him he translated the New Testament from Greek into Syriac, because of its variations, exactly as it was." The new revision had from the first a victorious career. Backed by the authority of the greatest

[1] See *S. Ephraim's Quotations from the Gospel* (Texts and Studies, vii. 2), p. 57.

ruler that Syriac-speaking Christianity has ever seen, it rapidly supplanted all its rivals, and only two fragmentary copies of the Old Syriac Gospels now survive. One is in the British Museum, where it was discovered and edited by Dr. Cureton, a former Canon of Westminster and Rector of S. Margaret's; the other is a Palimpsest in the Library of the Convent of S. Catherine on Mount Sinai. Both are very ancient; the Sinai Palimpsest probably dates from the fourth century, while Cureton's MS. is more probably of the fifth century, *i.e.* contemporary with Bishop Rabbula.

No 'Old Syriac' MS. of the Acts or Epistles has come down to us, and the Apocalypse forms no part of the Bible in Syriac.

But the analogy between the Latin and the Syriac Versions is not complete. There is nothing in the history of the Gospels in Latin to correspond with the influence of Tatian's *Diatessaron*. Tatian was an 'Assyrian,' *i.e.* a native of the Euphrates Valley, who studied at Rome in the middle of the second century under Justin Martyr. Towards the end of his career, about 173 A.D., his views were considered heretical at Rome, and he went back to his native land, where he died. It is not certain where he composed the *Diatessaron*, whether in Rome or in the East, and it is even disputed whether it was originally composed in Greek and translated into

Syriac, or whether it was originally composed in Syriac. But it was certainly the form in which the Gospel was most widely read by Syriac-speaking people up to the episcopate of Rabbula.

The *Diatessaron* is a Harmony, a sort of patchwork Gospel, in which an attempt was made to combine the Four Canonical Gospels into a single comprehensive narrative. It is curious how popular it was in the East. Theodoret, a contemporary of Rabbula of Edessa, and himself Bishop of a neighbouring See, tells us that he found "more than two hundred such books held in respect in the churches of our parts: and" (he adds) "I collected and put them all away and introduced the Gospels of the four Evangelists in their place."[1] The same process went on elsewhere, and so the *Diatessaron* went out of use. No copy of it seems ever to have reached the great Nitrian Library, the source from whence most of the Syriac MSS. in London and Rome have come, and even the Commentary which S. Ephraim wrote on the *Diatessaron* is extant only in an Armenian translation.

When we were attempting to sketch the history of the N.T. in Latin there were many blank intervals, but for the history of the N.T. in Syriac

[1] *Haer.* i. 20: τὰ τῶν τεττάρων εὐαγγελιστῶν ἀντεισήγαγον εὐαγγέλια.

from its beginning in the second century to the publication of the Peshitta in the fifth the materials simply do not exist. The 'Acts of Judas Thomas,' a religious romance written in Syriac some time in the third century, appears to quote the Gospel in a form akin to the Sinai Palimpsest and Cureton's MS. The other surviving remains of early Syriac literature up to Rabbula's time seem all to use the *Diatessaron*.[1]

The really important question, which seriously affects the date of the Old Syriac Version, is whether it is earlier or later than the first introduction of the *Diatessaron*. As I have just said, Tatian's work in the East lies between 170 and 180 A.D. That therefore is the date of the original Syriac Diatessaron. If the earliest Syriac Version of the Four Gospels be older than the Diatessaron, then that Syriac Version is exceedingly ancient, a true product of the second century. But if the Gospel was first brought to Syriac-speaking lands in the form of Tatian's Harmony, then the earliest Syriac Version may be no earlier than the middle of the third century.

[1] The list comprises the *Doctrine of Addai* (3rd cent.), the Syriac *Doctrine of the Apostles*, published by Cureton (3rd cent.), the Homilies of Aphraates (337-345 A.D.), the genuine works of S. Ephraim (died 373 A.D.), the Homilies of Cyrillona (fl. 400 A.D.). The Dialogue *De Fato* contains no quotation from the N.T.

This is a delicate critical question, and at present no definite conclusions have been attained. Till the discovery of the Sinai Palimpsest in 1893, the defenders of the priority of the Diatessaron had much the best of the argument. But the Sinai Palimpsest has in many respects a much better text than could have been anticipated from other Syriac evidence. It is, for instance, the only Syriac authority for the omission of the so-called 'last twelve verses' of S. Mark's Gospel. In many variations it supplies the reading from which the readings of other Syriac texts seem to have been ultimately derived, and it is free from the ascetic 'encratite' tendency which was generally characteristic of Syriac Christianity, a tendency which was sufficiently pronounced to make itself felt in other early Syriac texts of the Gospel. In a word, the Sinai Palimpsest appears to represent an earlier stage of Syriac Christianity than is represented by any other known document, except perhaps the Bardesanian Dialogue *De Fato*. Until these characteristics of the Sinai Palimpsest are explained away it will still be possible to believe that the 'Old Syriac' version of the Gospels, of which the Sinai Palimpsest is so faithful a descendant, is older than the Syriac Diatessaron—older, that is, than 170 A.D.

The Syriac Diatessaron often agrees with the Old Syriac in its renderings of the Greek, but there are many instances in which they differ, and it is quite possible that in their earliest forms they may have been more different still. It must not be forgotten also that only fragments of the Diatessaron survive, and these have to be gleaned from the Armenian translation of the Commentary of S. Ephraim and from S. Ephraim's own quotations and those of his contemporary, Aphraates. A striking instance of the difference between the two texts is to be found in Matt. xxvii. 16, 17, where the Old Syriac gives the name *Jesus* to Barabbas, Pilate saying, "Whom will ye that I release unto you—Jesus bar Abba, or Jesus called the Messiah?" But in the Diatessaron there is no trace of this interesting addition.

There are versions of the N.T. in other languages which may fairly be called ancient, but they are altogether on a later and lower plane than the Latin and Syriac. The history of the Egyptian or Coptic versions appears to be bound up with the development of Monastic life in the Christian Church: the earliest rendering of the N.T. into any Egyptian dialect may date from the end of the 3rd century or the beginning of the 4th.[1] The

[1] See especially the masterly tract by Ignazio Guidi called *Le Traduzioni dal Copto*, in the "Nachrichten von der K. Gesellschaft der Wissenschaften zu Göttingen" for 1889, pp. 49-56.

earliest Armenian and Georgian versions were made from the Syriac: what we now possess is a revision, made early in the 5th century by altering this earlier version into conformity with Greek MSS. Something similar appears to underlie the Ethiopic or Abyssinian version, but its history has not been properly made out. The Gothic version of Ulphilas, the earliest rendering of the Bible into any Teutonic dialect, is a product of the 4th century, and had a curious influence upon some of the later Latin texts current in N. Italy.

But the discussion of matters of this kind, though interesting in itself, has only a distant bearing upon the direct criticism of the New Testament. With the Latin and the Syriac in their earlier forms it is different. These versions are primary authorities for determining the sacred text. Where they agree we are listening to the *consensus* of the extreme East and the extreme West of the Roman world, speaking hardly more than a generation after the Four Gospels had been gathered together by the Church into one collection. Such a *consensus* is never to be disregarded, even though unsupported by a single surviving Greek MS. Let me give in conclusion a few instances of what I mean, a few instances where these early versions alone or almost alone preserve the true text of the Gospels.

In the opening words of the Parable of the Wise and Foolish Virgins we read, *Then shall the kingdom of heaven be likened unto ten virgins, which took their lamps and went forth to meet the bridegroom* (Matt. xxv. 1). This is the reading of nearly all our Greek MSS., including the oldest. But a few Greek authorities, supported by the Syriac and by the Latin versions, add at the end of the verse the words *and the bride.* The "Virgins" went forth "to meet the Bridegroom and the Bride." Now this addition gives a very graphic touch to the picture, while at the same time it is brought into better accordance with Oriental custom. The bridegroom goes with his friends to bring away the bride from her father's home;[1] no one is left at the bridegroom's dwelling but a few maidservants to keep the house. In the parable these maidservants represent the Church, while the arrival of the wedding procession with the bridegroom and his bride represents the coming of Christ. Christ is the bridegroom and the bride; the waiting servants are the Church.

But of all the stock of Christian imagery nothing was more familiar than the comparison of Christ to the Bridegroom and the Church to the Bride. Now

---

[1] See the account of that unlucky Wedding at Medaba, described in 1 Macc. ix. 37 ff., when through the attack of Jonathan and Simon the marriage was turned into mourning and the noise of their melody into lamentation.

it is the "Virgins" in the parable who obviously represent the Church; how then could they go forth to meet the Bride, the Spouse of Christ? When the Bride had become the stock metaphor for the Church, the careless scribe or editor had a strong temptation to leave it out in the parable where it does *not* mean the Church; and, as I said, this omission has actually been made in all but a very few of our Greek MSS. But the Latin and the Syriac versions kept the bride in the wedding procession, and we shall do well to replace her there.

In the preceding example we have been considering a case where the text familiar to us has lost a genuine and graphic detail, which has been preserved by the united testimony of nearly all our Latin and Syriac texts. I shall now give a couple of instances where a characteristic difference between parallel narratives has been obliterated in almost all our authorities by the insertion of words which properly belong to one Gospel into the text of another. In the cases which we are going to discuss, the true text, as I take it, has been preserved only in the Sinai Palimpsest, representing the Old Syriac Version in the East, and one Latin or Graeco-Latin text in the West.

S. Luke tells us that when the messengers of John the Baptist came to Jesus to ask whether He were indeed he that should come, Jesus replied,

Go your way, and tell John what things ye have seen and heard; the blind see, the lame walk, the lepers are cleansed, the deaf hear, the dead are raised up, the poor have the Gospel preached to them (Lk. vii. 22). There is no variation of any importance here in our MSS., and doubtless we have the verse very much as S. Luke penned it. The last clause is especially characteristic of the Third Evangelist—"the poor have the Gospel preached to them," or, as we may say to get nearer the Greek, "the poor are evangelised," πτωχοὶ εὐαγγελίζονται. It is S. Luke alone who tells us of the scene in the synagogue at Nazareth, where our Lord reads the passage of Isaiah which speaks about "preaching the Gospel to the poor" (Lk. iv. 18), and indeed this verb εὐαγγελίζεσθαι occurs ten times in his Gospel. It is therefore remarkable to find that the only passage in the other Gospels where the verb occurs is in the parallel passage in S. Matthew. According to the ordinary text, the answer of Christ to the disciples of John is the same in S. Matthew as in S. Luke (Matt. xi. 4, 5 = Lk. vii. 22). But Cod. Bobiensis (*k*), the best representation of the African Latin, and the Sinai Palimpsest, the best representative of the Old Syriac, in company with Clement of Alexandria[1] and (apparently) the *Diatessaron*[2]—

[1] *Paed.* I. x. 90 (151).

[2] See Ephraim's Commentary (*Moesinger*, 100).

these four alone among our authorities for the text—omit in S. Matthew the clause *πτωχοὶ εὐαγγελίζονται*, "the poor have the Gospel preached to them." I cannot doubt that they are right in so doing. The clause belongs to S. Luke, and is characteristic of his Gospel: it does not belong to S. Matthew, it is not characteristic of his Gospel, and its presence there would lead to very unsafe conclusions as to what was contained at this point in the common source of S. Matthew and S. Luke. We may reject the words, not on a ready-made theory of what ought or ought not to be in the Gospel according to S. Matthew, but upon the authority of the oldest Latin and the oldest Syriac texts.

One more instance and I have done. Whatever theories we may hold about the authorship and composition of the Fourth Gospel, the Gospel according to S. John, one thing is clear: the Evangelist was the very reverse of anxious to make his diction harmonise verbally with the other Gospels. Very few of the sayings of Jesus in the Gospel according to S. John are given in the other Gospels also. So much is this the case, that many students of the Fourth Gospel, both in ancient and in modern times, have supposed that the Evangelist actually avoided what had been already told: his aim was to supply the lines previously left out in the Portrait of the Lord.

In this Gospel there is an account of a supper at Bethany where Martha served and Mary anointed the feet of Jesus. The story appears also to be told in S. Mark and S. Matthew, but with many variations of time and circumstance. The account in the Fourth Gospel must have been based on quite a different tradition, and accordingly the words of our Lord are given differently. One sentence, however, is the same in S. Mark and S. John, as given in almost all our authorities: this is *For the poor ye have always with you, but me ye have not always* (Joh. xii. 8 = Mk. xiv. 7, Matt. xxvi. 11). The sudden verbal agreement in the midst of so much material divergence is extremely striking. It is therefore a matter of no ordinary interest to those who are studying the mutual relations of our Gospels to find that the words I have just quoted are omitted from the text of S. John in the Sinai Palimpsest and in the Graeco-Latin Codex Bezae (D), our great 5th century MS. at Cambridge. According to this our Lord's only answer to the complaint of Judas is, *Suffer her to keep it against the day of my burying*. The removal of the words about the poor takes away the sudden and inexplicable literary resemblance at this point between S. John and the Synoptic Gospels: here again, therefore, we may believe that the Syriac Palimpsest from the East and the Graeco-Latin MS. from the

West have preserved the true text. These two have remained free from a harmonistic interpolation which has invaded the rest of the extant texts of the Fourth Gospel.

These three instances will, I trust, sufficiently illustrate the main point of what I have attempted to say this afternoon. We have seen that owing to the political conditions of the Roman Empire the New Testament was very early translated from the Greek into two languages, and into two only—Latin in the West and Syriac in the East. These versions may be placed with confidence in the 2nd century; it is doubtful whether the Bible was translated into any other language before the early years of the 4th century. Our Latin and Syriac MSS. are not older than the end of the 4th century, but in spite of later revision from the Greek some of them do contain a fairly faithful image of the original translation. By the help of these early translations, and especially where East and West agree, we are often able to restore the true text in places where our Greek MSS. give a perverted reading. The Latin Church of Roman Africa and the Syriac Church of Edessa have both of them perished, but through their vernacular versions of the New Testament they being dead yet speak to us.

The History of the Canon of the New Testament.

Characteristics of the History.—Four influences: (1) Christian worship; (2) Literary habit; (3) Translation; (4) Controversy (Gnostic sects; the Muratorian Fragment).

The evidence of Eusebius as to the Canon ('the acknowledged Books,' 'the disputed Books'). The two periods of the History.

I. The period till about 200 A.D. Range of the N.T. Canon at the close of this period; Irenaeus (reasons for the importance of his evidence); the N.T. of Irenaeus. Recognition of Books and of groups of Books.

(1) The collection of the Four Gospels. Irenaeus; the Shepherd of Hermas; Heracleon; Tatian's Diatessaron; Justin Martyr (Papias).

(2) The Acts of the Apostles.

(3) The Pauline Epistles. Irenaeus; Theophilus of Antioch; Marcion; Polycarp and Ignatius.

II. The period 200—400 A.D.

(1) The Epistle to the Hebrews. (*a*) Eastern Churches: Pantaenus, Clement, Origen, Eusebius; the Syriac Vulgate; the Antiochene School; Amphilochius. (*b*) Western Churches: Clement of Rome; Hippolytus; Muratorian Fragment; Caius; Irenaeus; Tertullian, Cyprian, the 'Cheltenham' list; Jerome; Augustine.

(2) The Apocalypse. (*a*) Irenaeus; Theophilus; Melito of Sardis; Justin Martyr. (*b*) Influence of Montanism; Caius; the Alogi; Dionysius of Alexandria; (*c*) Eastern (Greek) Churches; Western Churches.

Reasons for divergence of earlier and later views.

(3) The Catholic Epistles. Early Syriac Church ('Doctrine of Addai').

(α) 1 Peter, 1 John.

(β) James, 1 Peter, 1 John. Reception of James into the Canon.

(γ) James, 1 Peter, 1 John, 2, 3 John, Jude, 2 Peter.

Reception of Jude into the Canon; about 200 A.D.; Origen; Carthage; reasons for later doubts (Didymus, Jerome).

Reception of 2 Peter into the Canon; lack of early references; Origen (Clement); the Fourth Century; causes of its reception.

Recognition of the full Canon of N.T. in (1) Eastern (Greek) Churches; (2) Western Churches.

Conclusion.

The History of the growth of the Canon of the New Testament is a complicated subject. Its full discussion presupposes some knowledge of the history of the early Church and of the characteristics and the environment of the chief writers in the first centuries; and it involves a somewhat minute investigation of references, or supposed references, in the Fathers to the words of the New Testament. One brief lecture, therefore, must necessarily leave unsaid very much even of what lies on the surface of the subject. Not seldom statements may seem obscure to those who are not familiar with the outlines of Church History. And, what is perhaps even more important, any discussion of different interpretations of the evidence must be ruthlessly excluded. We must keep to the main road, and not allow ourselves to be allured into bye-paths however attractive.

The Canon of the New Testament is the collection of those Books which have been recognized by the general opinion of Christian men as apostolic and therefore as authoritative.

The word Canon in application to the Sacred Books may be taken (1) in a passive sense, as signifying the list of Books which are marked out; or (2) in an active sense, as denoting those Books which themselves mark out the rule of Christian faith and life. We need not stop to discuss the question which of these two conceptions is the more original. Both of them were probably in early times connected with the term.

The history of the formation of the Canon is the history not of a series of events but of a long continuous process. The Canon is not, as we might have expected, the outcome of any definite decision. It was never the subject of any ordinance of a General Council. Like the Apostles' Creed, it was the result, gradually and informally attained, of the activity of the Christian consciousness, of the thought and the practice of the whole body of the Faithful.

This process of a selection of certain Books from a larger number and their recognition as a 'divine library' was not new. It was indeed a repetition—we may almost say a continuation. The Christian Church inherited from the Jewish Church the Old Testament as its earliest Bible, and the completion of the Canon of the Old Testament did not belong to a distant past. "The measure of the completeness of the Canon had scarcely been reached, when 'the fulness of the time came.' The close of the Hebrew Canon brings us to the threshold of the Christian Church. The history of the Canon, like the teaching of its inspired contents, leads us into the very presence of Him in Whom alone we have the fulfilment and the interpretation of the Old Testament, and the one perfect sanction for its use."[1]

Taking a broad view of the history of the Canon of the New Testament, we may say that four influences were at work.

(1) THE CUSTOM OF CHRISTIAN WORSHIP.—The assemblies for Christian worship grew out of, and were modelled upon, the worship of the Synagogues. In the Synagogue lessons from the Law and the Prophets were read, and were followed by a 'discourse of exhortation.'[2] In the earliest times in the Christian assemblies an Epistle just received from an Apostle would be read (1 Thess. v. 27, Col. iv. 16; comp. Eus. *H.E.* IV. 23), and the place of the exhortation, we may conjecture, taken by an account of some part of our Lord's teaching, or of the Passion or the Resurrection. In the first half of the second century at Rome, as we learn from Justin Martyr (*Ap.* i. 67), "the Memoirs of the Apostles, [*i.e.* the Gospels] or the writings of the Prophets [were] read." Thus Christian people grew accus-

[1] Bp. Ryle, *The Canon of the Old Testament*, preface, p. ix. f.

[2] Schürer, *History of the Jewish People*, *Eng. Trans.*, II. ii. p. 82. Compare Luke iv. 17 ff., Acts xiii. 15 ff.

tomed to regard the Apostolic writings as 'Scripture,' in the same sense as the Old Testament; and liturgical custom, varying doubtless in different churches, set its seal on certain Christian Books and groups of Books as worthy of special reverence and obedience.

(2) Literary Habit.—As time went on, a Christian literature grew in volume and was circulated in the different churches. Christian writers wove into their own written words the familiar phrases of the Apostolic writers, and in a few cases expressly quoted them. Thus they registered the decisions of popular usage; they tended to co-ordinate the customs of different churches and to give them permanence.

(3) Translation.—In the second century it became necessary to translate the Apostolic Books, written in Greek, into Syriac and into Latin, possibly also into the native dialects of Egypt. The range of Books so translated formed a Canon of the New Testament in these districts.

(4) Controversy.—When heresies arose and heretical sects became organized bodies, when the controversy between these sects and the Catholic Church found expression in tracts and treatises, the question as to the limits of the authoritative Books became a pressing one. The sects claimed that they represented the true tradition of the Apostles. The Catholic Church challenged and denied the claim.

The question thus arose, to what Books in this dispute could appeal be made? Hence Councils in particular Churches, as some evidence shews,[1] discussed the matter; and individual writers with more or less formality and definiteness expressed their opinion. In this way the general voice of the Catholic Church, *i.e.* the different local churches throughout the world which were in communion with each other, and from which the sects had broken away, was both expressed and controlled.

To one such definite statement it will be convenient to refer at this point—the Muratorian fragment. It derives its name from the Italian scholar, Muratori, who published it in 1740. It is evidently a rude Latin translation of a Greek original. That original was probably drawn up at Rome late in the second century. Bishop Lightfoot[2] has made it probable that the original Greek was written in verse as a kind of *memoria technica*, and that the writer was Hippolytus, a learned and voluminous author, who seems as Bishop to have presided over the foreign congregations at Rome. The Books of the New Testament which are explicitly recognized in it are

---

[1] Si non ab omni concilio ecclesiarum etiam vestrarum inter apocrypha et falsa judicaretur (*Tert. de Pudic.* x.). Tertullian is speaking as a Montanist to Catholic Christians; hence the word 'vestrarum.'

[2] *St. Clement of Rome,* ii. pp. 405 ff.

the following: the four Gospels, the Acts, the Pauline Epistles (not including the Epistle to the Hebrews), the Apocalypse of St. John, and two, if not the three, Epistles of St. John.[1]

The Muratorian Fragment illustrates several important points. (*a*) It shews with what interest and care the question of the Canon, to use the later term, was treated at the end of the second century in the Church at Rome—a Church naturally

[1] In reference to the Gospel of St. John, the writer notes how "firmly John sets forth each statement [about the Lord] in his Epistle also," quoting 1 John i. 1 ff. Later in the Fragment, after mentioning the Epistle of St. Jude, he refers to "the couple [of Epistles] bearing the name of John" as "accepted in the Catholic Church." The context seems to suggest that 'the couple' are the two short Epistles which bears St. John's name. If this interpretation is correct, the three Epistles of St. John are included in the Muratorian list.

Neither of the Epistles which bear the name of St. Peter have a place in the Fragment as it stands. The Fragment, however, is mutilated at the beginning; it commences in the middle of a sentence which clearly concluded what the writer had to say about St. Mark. It is highly probable that, just as the writer mentioned 1 John in connexion with St. John's Gospel, so, in the portion of his work now lost which dealt with St. Mark, he quoted 1 Pet. v. 13 in reference to St. Mark's relation to St. Peter at Rome, as Papias appears to have done. It should be added that Prof. Zahn restores a passage of the Fragment thus (the words which he adds being in square brackets): "The Apocalypse also of John, and of Peter [one Epistle, which] only we receive: [there is also a second] which some of our friends will not have read in the Church." But such a restoration cannot be regarded as more than an ingenious conjecture.

regarded by other churches as a centre and as a standard (Iren. iii. 3). (*b*) It shews how it was under the pressure of controversy that what was a matter of devotional instinct and usage became a matter of formal discussion. The Fragment is evidently a controversial document. It mentions by name certain heretics, together with the books which they held sacred, and with these heretics it contrasts the Catholic Church, from whose collection of Apostolic Books the books of the sects must be rigorously excluded. "For," it is said, "it is not fitting that honey be mixed with gall." (*c*) It shews that the formation of the Canon was a process of selection. The need of excluding the books of the sectaries called attention to the question of certain orthodox books which were challenging admission within the circle of authoritative Scriptures—*The Shepherd* of Hermas, to mention only one of these, the Pilgrim's Progress of the early Church, a book actually quoted as Scripture by Irenaeus (iv. 20). "The Shepherd," so the Fragment decides the claim, "ought indeed to be read [*i.e.* studied in private], but it cannot to the end of time be publicly read in the Church to the people, either among the Prophets, whose number is complete, or among the Apostles."

Such were in the main the influences which conditioned the gradual process whereby the Books of the New Testament were placed in a unique position of sacredness and of authority. The history of the Canon is not a matter of dry and legal research. It only needs an effort of the historical imagination, and we see that it is closely related to the daily life of our elder brethren in Christ. We picture them in the assemblies for worship, reading, listening, preaching; at home studying, and in a few cases writing; and so gradually coming to recognize and to use the same New Testament which we recognize and use to-day. The formation of the Canon was an element, one of the most important and fruitful elements, in the devotional life of the early Church.

But it is time to go into detail. The best starting point for an historical review of the collection of the several groups of Books is the well-known passage, or pair of passages, in the *Ecclesiastical History* of Eusebius, in which he deals with the subject of the Canon (*H.E.* iii. 3, 25). The life of Eusebius extended approximately from 270 to 340 A.D. Early in the fourth century he witnessed the horrors of the last great persecution. It was a characteristic of this final crusade of the empire against the Church that its leaders followed the statesman-like policy of endeavouring to destroy the sacred buildings and the sacred Books of the Church. "With mine own eyes," writes Eusebius (*H.E.* viii. 2), "I beheld the

Houses of Prayer being plucked down and razed to the ground, and the divine and sacred Scriptures in the public market places being consigned to the flames." This policy of *Thorough* had an effect in regard to the subject under discussion far indeed from the persecutors' intention. It raised the practical question what were the Books which no Christian man, in simple loyalty to his faith, could surrender to the enemy. Eusebius had doubtless faced this question; and his statements as to the limits of the Canon cannot but embody the opinions which he and his fellow-Christians formed at the dreadful crisis of the Diocletian persecution. In order to estimate aright the significance of Eusebius' treatment of the Canon, we must further remember that, as a leading Bishop in the years which lay on either side of the Council of Nicæa, and as the spiritual adviser of Constantine, he was brought into contact with nearly all the prominent ecclesiastics of the time, and was well acquainted with contemporary thought; and moreover, that, deficient as he was in the power of arranging and interpreting facts, his knowledge of the Christian literature of times earlier than his own was practically exhaustive.

Eusebius, then, divides those Christian writings which had any sort of claim to be reckoned among the Scriptures of the New Covenant into three groups. Below the lowest of these three groups, the spurious books (*e.g.* the *Acts of Paul*, the *Apocalypse of Peter*), there is a yet inferior class, the heretical books (*e.g.* the *Gospel of Peter*, the *Acts of John*). With these two lowest groups we need not further concern ourselves.

The highest group consists of the Books which are 'acknowledged,' *i.e.* 'the holy quaternion of the Gospels,' the Acts, the Epistles of St. Paul (including the Epistle to the Hebrews, though, as Eusebius notes elsewhere (*H.E.* iii. 3), some had rejected it inasmuch as its Pauline authorship had been disputed by the Roman Church, and though he himself elsewhere (*H.E.* vi. 13) includes it among the 'disputed books'). "Next to these," Eusebius continues, "we must maintain the current former Epistle of John, and likewise that of Peter." The list ends with the Apocalypse of John, though a note of hesitation is added; and in fact he also mentions the Apocalypse, here also with an expression of uncertainty, among the 'spurious' books.

The second group comprehends those Books "which are disputed but which are nevertheless familiar to most persons"—"the so-called Epistle of James," that of Jude, the Second Epistle of Peter, and "the so-called Second and Third Epistles of John, whether they be the work of the Evangelist or it may be of some other John."

These two groups—the 'acknowledged' and the

'disputed Books'—correspond to the two periods into which the whole history of the Canon may be divided. The earlier period reaches from the date of rise of an Apostolic literature to the end of the second or the beginning of the third century. The later period comprises the third and fourth centuries. We will consider the two periods separately.

I. During the earlier period the 'acknowledged Books' gained their pre-eminent position. In the first place the separate Books were recognized as Apostolic and authoritative. Secondly, the Gospels and the Epistles of St. Paul were formed into collections, and these collections were co-ordinated with the Canon of the Old Testament. Before we trace the growth of these collections of Books, it is important that we should recognize how clear and convincing the testimony is as to the supreme position held towards the close of this period by the Gospels, the Acts, the Pauline Epistles, the First Epistles of St. Peter and of St. John respectively, and the Apocalypse.

In the first three quarters of the second century the literature of the Christian Church was unsystematic and limited. It consists chiefly of letters and apologies, the latter being treatises addressed to those without, in which, from the very nature of the case, there was but little opportunity for quotations from, or direct references to, the Apostolic writings. But during the last twenty years of the century a strictly theological literature arose in the Church. Thus at Alexandria we have the voluminous works of Clement; at Carthage the no less voluminous and the even more varied works of Tertullian, the earliest Latin writer of Christendom; at Lyons in South Gaul the controversial treatise of Irenaeus. I take the last named, Irenaeus, as a type. What is said of him in regard to his use of the Books of the New Testament might, I believe, be said with equal truth of Clement and of Tertullian.

The character of the treatise of Irenaeus which has come down to us is sufficiently clear from the title "Of the Refutation and Overthrow of Knowledge falsely so-called Five Books." It is directed against the Gnostics, those, that is, who claimed to be an aristocracy in regard to knowledge (gnosis). The treatise can be dated with considerable precision. The third book was written while Eleutherus was Bishop of Rome, *i.e.* before the year 190 A.D. Irenaeus, whose life extended approximately from 130 to 200 A.D., is a writer of extreme importance, for several reasons.

(*a*) His is the first book on a large scale in which a Christian speaks to Christians and deals with matters of Christian doctrine; the first, that is, in which we should expect a detailed and explicit appeal to the Apostolic literature.

(*b*) Irenaeus was a travelled man. Like Ulysses "he had seen the cities of many men and known their mind." A native of Asia Minor, he lived and lectured in Rome, and afterwards became Bishop of Lyons. Thus he delivers his judgments, knowing the opinions and the customs of different churches; and his views on such a matter as the Books of the New Testament could not be divergent from those generally held. His judgment is not the mere judgment of an individual writer.

(*c*) Irenaeus was the pupil of Polycarp, Bishop of Smyrna, who in 155 A.D. at the age of eighty-six suffered martyrdom at Smyrna. Polycarp was a disciple of St. John. A letter is preserved by Eusebius (*H.E.* v. 20), in which Irenaeus reminds a fellow-pupil of his of their common master, Polycarp, "how he would describe his intercourse with John and with the rest who had seen the Lord, and how he would recount their words. And whatsoever things he had heard from them about the Lord, and about His miracles, and about His teaching, Polycarp, as having received them from eyewitnesses of the life of the Word, would relate altogether in accordance with the Scriptures." You will note in the last sentence the meeting point of the two streams, oral tradition and Scriptural testimony. Thus Irenaeus is a link with those Apostles who, apparently after the destruction of Jerusalem, settled in Asia Minor, St. John, St. Philip, St. Andrew. Through Polycarp, Irenaeus is the spiritual grandson of St. John.

What then was the New Testament of Irenaeus? I answer in the words of Bishop Lightfoot: "The authority which Irenaeus attributes to the four Gospels, the Acts of the Apostles, the Epistles of St. Paul, several of the Catholic Epistles, and the Apocalypse, falls short in no respect of the estimate of the Church Catholic in the fourth or the ninth or the nineteenth century. He treats them as on a level with the Canonical Books of the Old Testament; he cites them as Scripture in the same way; he attributes them to the respective authors whose names they bear; he regards them as writings handed down in the several Churches from the beginning; he fills his page with quotations from them; he has not only a very thorough knowledge of their contents himself, but he assumes an acquaintance with and a recognition of them in his readers."[1]

We turn then now to the recognition during this period of the Collection of the Four Gospels, of the Acts of the Apostles, and of the Collection of the Pauline Epistles.

[1] *Essays on the work entitled Supernatural Religion*, pp. 261 ff.

(1) The Four Gospels.—We start with a well-known passage of Irenaeus (iii. 11, ed. Massuet). Irenaeus points out that different Gnostic sects selected different Gospels as supplying an apostolic confirmation of their peculiar tenets. The Ebionites, he says, used only St. Matthew; the Marcionites only St. Luke (in a mutilated form); another sect who separated Jesus and the Christ—the human, that is, and the Divine in the Lord—only St. Mark; the Valentinians only St. John. When, then, their separate testimonies are combined, the sects support the four Gospels of the Catholic Church. But indeed, he continues, the Gospels cannot in the nature of things be either more or less than four in number. The number *four* is stamped upon creation. There are *four* quarters of the world; *four* great winds. It is natural and reasonable, therefore, that, as the Church is spread throughout the earth and the Gospel is the support of the Church, the Church should have *four* pillars. Moreover, there are *four* catholic covenants, those given to Noah, Abraham, Moses, and that given to man through Jesus Christ. And yet again, the Word, the Creator of all things, is represented in the Psalm (lxxx. 1) as seated on the Cherubim, and the Cherubim are four-faced, When the Word was manifested to men, He bestowed on us "the Gospel in a fourfold form.

yet bound together by one Spirit." Irenaeus, we may note in passing, presents here the earliest interpretation of the evangelical symbols. The lion prefigures St. John's Gospel, the calf that of St. Luke, the man that of St. Matthew, the eagle that of St. Mark.

The analogies on which Irenaeus relies seem to us fanciful; the argument drawn from them is altogether insecure. But the importance of the passage does not lie in its logical cogency, but rather in this—it is clear evidence that Irenaeus regarded the four Gospels as we do to-day, as holding a unique place. He cannot imagine the Church without the four Gospels, or with Gospels less or more than four in number.

But this parabolic language as to the Four Gospels was probably no invention of Irenaeus. It was not, it seems, original. Origen, writing some years later, speaks of the four Gospels as the elements of the Church's faith, "of which elements the whole world is compacted" (*In Joan.* i. 6). The passage in Origen is very similar, yet it is not precisely parallel, to the passage in Irenaeus; and it is exceedingly probable, though it perhaps cannot be said to be certain, that both these writers derived their conception of the fourfold Gospel from a yet earlier writer, Hermas. In one of the visions of the *Shepherd* of Hermas (iii. 13), Hermas sees a lady, who had before appeared to him as an aged woman, now young and fair. "And since thou sawest her seated on a couch, her position is firm; for the couch hath four feet and standeth firmly; for the world too is upheld by means of four elements." The lady in the vision is the Church of God; the four feet of the couch are almost certainly the four Gospels. This interpretation of the imagery is strongly confirmed by the context, in which Hermas speaks of *good tidings* (ἀγγελία ἀγαθή τις) coming to one in sorrow, so that his spirit is renewed by reason of his joy: "even so," he adds, "you also have received a renewal of your spirits by seeing these good things." Now the date of the *Shepherd* is about the middle of the second century, so that, if this interpretation of its imagery is correct, the evidence for the collection of the four Gospels is carried back some forty or fifty years earlier than the time when Irenaeus wrote.

But this evidence does not stand alone. About the year 170 Heracleon, a leader of one of the Gnostic sects, wrote a commentary on St. John's Gospel and, as it appears, on that of St. Luke also. Even in the fragments of his work which still survive we discover several references to St. Matthew. The consideration that Heracleon deals with the *words* rather than with the life of Christ, and that St.

Mark records little of Christ's teaching which is not found in the other Synoptists, sufficiently accounts for the fact that these fragments contain no allusion to any words characteristic of the second Gospel. We must not fail to remark that a commentary, and the use in that commentary of allegorical methods of interpretation, imply the attribution to the Books expounded of an authority long recognized.

About the same time Tatian, a writer who belonged to another Gnostic sect, drew up a harmony of the four Gospels called the Diatessaron, *i.e.* the History of the Lord told by four writers. Evidence which has come to light during the last twenty-five years leaves us in no doubt as to the character of Tatian's work.[1] He used our four Gospels just as a harmonist of to-day might use them. The fact of the compilation of such a Harmony in itself speaks volumes. But Tatian's Harmony was not in Greek, the original language of the four Gospels, but in Syriac. This implies that the four Gospels had been already translated into Syriac; and translation is a tribute to the recognized authority of the work translated, and moreover implies that it is no literary upstart. Thus the Harmony of Tatian is a testimony to the supreme position which the Gospels

[1] See *e.g.* Hamlyn Hill's *The Earliest Life of Christ, being the Diatessaron of Tatian.*

must long have held as the authoritative records of the Life of Christ.

But we can go a step further back. Probably a few years *before* the middle of the second century, Justin Martyr at Rome addressed to the Emperor Antoninus Pius his defence of Christianity, and about the same time wrote his Dialogue with the Jew Trypho, a controversial treatise against the Jews. In these apologetic works, addressed to those without, Justin avoids the use of terms which were characteristic of the Christian Church. Referring to the records of the Lord's Life, he employs a word which, as the title of Xenophon's account of Socrates, was familiar to educated men—'the Memoirs,' 'the Memoirs of the Apostles.' But in one passage (*Ap.* i. 66) he is more explicit and speaks of 'the Memoirs' written by the Apostles "which are called Gospels." These 'Memoirs,' he tells us, no doubt with special reference to the custom of the Roman Church, were publicly read. "On the so-called day of the Sun there is a meeting of all of us who live in cities or in the country, and the Memoirs of the Apostles or the writings of the Prophets are read, so long as time allows" (*Ap.* i. 67). The works of Justin contain allusions to the Lord's words and works of such a kind as to imply the use of each one of the four Gospels. Moreover, in one passage (*Dial.* 103), speaking of 'the Memoirs,' Justin adds "which I assert to have been drawn up by His Apostles and by those who followed them." In both cases you will observe that the plural is used. This statement as to the authorship of 'the Memoirs' precisely agrees with the case of our four Gospels—two bearing the name of Apostles (St. Matthew, St. John), two the names of followers of the Apostles (St. Mark, St. Luke). If we still hesitate as to the identification of Justin's 'Memoirs of the Apostles' with our four Gospels, we recall the fact that Tatian, who drew up a Harmony of the four Gospels, was the pupil of Justin.

The last witness to whom we appeal speaks with a less decisive voice. Papias of Hierapolis, whose life (to give the probable limits of date) extended from 65 to 135 A.D., is a Subapostolic Father of extreme importance. He had seen and known some of those who had seen and known the Lord. He was the author of a treatise of five books on 'the Oracles of the Lord,' of which Eusebius (*H.E.* iii. 39) quotes fragments of great interest, which however are sadly scanty. Papias, then, in the fragments preserved by Eusebius, explicitly refers to the Gospels according to St. Matthew[1] and St. Mark, giving important details

[1] It is right to quote the actual words of Papias as preserved by Eusebius—"So then Matthew composed the Oracles in the Hebrew language, and each one translated them as he was able."

as to their composition. But what of St. John and St. Luke? Eusebius informs us that Papias used (*i.e.* in a portion of his work which has not come down to us) testimonies from the First Epistle of St. John. The Epistle and the Gospel of St. John are so closely related that knowledge and acceptance of the one implies knowledge and acceptance of the other. Moreover, there are, as Bishop Lightfoot has shewn,[1] independent reasons for holding that Papias knew and used the fourth Gospel. The case

---

On this Mr. W. C. Allen (*Contentio Veritatis*, p. 210) writes thus: "It is clear that this statement cannot apply to our Gospel as it now exists. It is not written in Hebrew, nor is it a translation of a Hebrew work. And the term *Logia*, i.e. *Oracles*, or *Sayings*, would be a very unsuitable word to describe so carefully articulated a theological treatise in narrative form as our Gospel." But it must be observed that it may well be that Eusebius does not give the whole of what Papias said about St. Matthew, just as it is certain from the words which he quotes that he does not give the whole of what Papias said about St. Mark. In the words "each one translated them" (notice the past tense) Papias clearly refers to a state of things which had passed away when he wrote. It would be natural and almost inevitable that he should continue the history and explain how it was that the need for individual translation had, when he wrote, ceased to exist. Further, Bishop Lightfoot (*Essays on Supernatural Religion*, pp. 172 ff.; comp. Bishop Westcott, *Canon*, p. 73 n.) shews that the term *Oracles* was, as a matter of fact, used to include narratives as well as discourses. It is remarkable, and not without significance, that Mr. Allen passes over the work of Bishop Westcott and Bishop Lightfoot (*e.g.* on the Fourth Gospel) as though it did not exist.

[1] *Essays on the work entitled Supernatural Religion*, pp. 192 ff.

of St. Luke is different. There is some evidence which makes it probable that Papias was acquainted with the Gospel of St. Luke, but it is slight and inconclusive. Proof, therefore, just stops short of allowing us to assert that Papias acknowledged the fourfold Gospel. If we could with confidence have appealed to Papias, we should have traced the evidence for the collection of the four Gospels to the first quarter of the first century. As the case stands, we must stop short at the name of Justin Martyr; and his testimony warrants us in saying that in the second quarter of the first century the four Gospels as a collection of Books had already secured a unique position of authority in the Church.

(2) THE ACTS OF THE APOSTLES.—Of the Acts it must suffice to say that at the end of the period the Book is referred to by the title familiar to ourselves—The Acts of the Apostles—and as the work of St. Luke. This is the case with Irenaeus, Bishop of Lyons (iii. 13. 3), with the author of the Muratorian Canon, speaking from Rome; with Clement of Alexandria (*Strom.* v. 12, p. 696 ed. Potter); with Tertullian of Carthage (*adv. Marc.* v. 1, *de Jejun.* 10). Two further observations must be added. Earlier writers incorporate language drawn from the Book. Again, since the Acts and the Gospel of St. Luke are clearly the work of the same author, and the two Books form a single whole, the evidence

which we have adduced of the acceptance of the Gospel in the second quarter of the second century implies the acceptance of the Acts.

(3) THE PAULINE EPISTLES.—We have seen how towards the end of the century Irenaeus quotes all the thirteen Epistles of St. Paul, with the one exception of the brief private letter to Philemon. Some ten years earlier Theophilus of Antioch wrote three books of 'Elementary Instruction,' in which he endeavoured to win over to the faith a learned heathen friend, Autolycus. In this treatise he quotes eight of St. Paul's Epistles, adducing a text from 1 Tim. as 'the divine word' (*Ad Autol.* iii. 14). A more important witness is Marcion, the Gnostic. Marcion, as a younger contemporary of Justin Martyr, takes us back well within the second quarter of the second century. He held St. Paul to be the only true Apostle, and, as we know from Tertullian and Epiphanius, accepted as authoritative *ten Epistles* of that Apostle. We can hardly doubt that he was influenced in his rejection of the Pastoral Epistles by controversial reasons. Those Epistles contain much which was clean opposed to Marcion's characteristic tenets, *e.g.* his views on marriage. From Clement of Alexandria (*Strom.* ii. 11, ed. Potter p. 457) we learn that certain heretics—not improbably he means the followers of Marcion—finding themselves convicted by the words, 'the objections

of knowledge falsely so-called,' rejected the Epistles to Timothy. Thus, in regard to the three Pastoral Epistles, Marcion's position is probably the exception which proves the rule of their acceptance. But however that may be, it remains true that Marcion supplies us with a very early instance of a Canon of Christian Scriptures, and that, though he freely handled the knife, he yet accepted as a collection *ten* of St. Paul's Epistles.

But we can trace the collection of St. Paul's Epistles to an earlier date. Polycarp of Smyrna in his letter to the Philippians, and Ignatius of Antioch in his seven letters to the Churches of Asia Minor and of Rome, incorporate the language of so many of St. Paul's Epistles, including the Pastoral Epistles, that it appears to be a legitimate inference that the complete collection of St. Paul's Epistles was in their hands. The witness of Polycarp and Ignatius brings us back to the year 115 A.D.[1] When they wrote the Pauline collection was already recognized in the Church.

II. We now turn to the second great period with which we have to deal, the third and fourth centuries. Our task is to trace the history of the acceptance of the Epistle to the Hebrews, of the Apocalypse, and of the collection of Epistles known as the Catholic

[1] These passages are collected on p. 183.

Epistles ; and finally, to shew under what influences the complete Canon of the New Testament was accepted in the East and in the West.

(1) THE EPISTLE TO THE HEBREWS.—There was in the early centuries a division of opinion as to the authorship, and consequently as to the authority, of this Epistle. The line of cleavage coincided with the natural boundary which separated Eastern from Western Christendom.

We turn then to the East, and in the East first to the Church of Alexandria. We have the witness of three generations of great Alexandrian teachers. Clement, as his words are preserved by Eusebius (*H.E.* vi. 14. 4), records how 'the blessed Elder'—doubtless his own master Pantaenus—'used to say' that St. Paul abstained from calling himself the 'Apostle of the Hebrews,' partly out of reverence for the Lord—for "He was the Apostle of the Almighty, and was sent to the Hebrews"—and partly because his writing to the Hebrews was outside his own proper work, "inasmuch as he was the herald and Apostle of the nations." The master then held that the Epistle was properly the work of St. Paul. The position of the pupil was somewhat different. Clement (*ap.* Eus. *H.E.* vi. 14. 2) maintained that St. Paul wrote the Epistle to the Hebrews in Hebrew, and refrained from adding his name because his countrymen were prejudiced against him, and that St. Luke translated the Hebrew original for the sake of Greek readers; hence the similarity in style between the Hebrews and the Acts. Origen, to pass to the next generation, notices the difference in style between this Epistle and those of St. Paul, though the thoughts are the thoughts of the Apostle. The conclusion to which he was led was that the Epistle was the composition of some one who recalled from memory St. Paul's teaching. "If any church, therefore, receive this Epistle as the Epistle of St. Paul, let it be applauded for this. For not without reason have those of old time handed the Epistle down as that of Paul. Howbeit who wrote the Epistle, God only knows the truth; but the account which has reached us is that Clement, as some say, or Luke, as others say, wrote it."[1] Thus Clement and Origen uphold the Pauline character rather than the Pauline authorship. Eusebius is not altogether consistent in his treatment of the question. In one place (*H.E.* vi. 13) he reckons this Epistle as one of the 'disputed Books'; in another passage (*H.E.* iii. 25) among the 'acknowledged Books'; elsewhere again (*H.E.* iii. 3) he mentions that some rejected it on the ground that the Church of Rome questioned it as not being the work of St. Paul. In a fourth passage (*H.E.* iii. 38) he records the opinion that St. Paul wrote to his own countrymen in their

[1] Ap. Eus. *H.E.* vi. 25. 11-14.

own language, adding that some who held this view taught that St. Luke, others that Clement of Rome, translated the Epistle into Greek, he himself inclining to the name of Clement. The Syriac Vulgate, the Peshitta, may be taken as not unfairly representing the general conclusion of earlier times. In that version the Epistle is simply called 'the Epistle to the Hebrews,' and it has a place immediately after St. Paul's Epistles; thus it is a kind of appendix to the Pauline group. Of the fourth century little need be said. In the lists of Cyril of Jerusalem and of Athanasius the Epistles of St. Paul are regarded as fourteen in number, and therefore as including that to the Hebrews. The great exegetes of the Antiochene School — Chrysostom and Theodore of Mopsuestia—commented on it as undoubtedly the work of St. Paul. Amphilochius of Iconium, in his list of New Testament Books, records and condemns the scepticism of some — "some say that that to the Hebrews is spurious, wrongly; for genuine is its grace." Thus in the East the Epistle to the Hebrews was accounted Pauline, but commonly, at least in earlier days, in a secondary sense.

In the West, Clement, writing at Rome in the year 95 A.D., shews his acquaintance with the Epistle; his mind, it is clear, was saturated with its ideas and words. A century later the case had altogether changed. Hippolytus, we are told (Photius *Cod.* 232), asserted that the Epistle was not St. Paul's, nor does he quote it in his extant works. It is omitted in the Muratorian Fragment. In a disputation held with Proclus, a Montanist leader, Caius, a Roman presbyter, appealed to thirteen Epistles of St. Paul, "not reckoning that to the Hebrews with the rest" (Eus. *H.E.* vi. 20). The contrast between the position of Clement and that of the Church at Rome a century later may in part be due to the fact that, after the Church had outgrown the traditions of the early period when its relations with the synagogue were more or less close, any relic of Jewish Christianity became distasteful to its members. But Rome in this matter was not isolated from other Western Churches. Only two MSS. remain, and those closely related to each other, which give an old Latin text of this Epistle. As to Irenaeus in South Gaul, though, according to Eusebius (*H.E.* v. 26), in a volume of 'divers discourses' he adduced passages from this Epistle, yet in his extant works, though it would have served his controversial purposes, he appears never to quote it. At Carthage Tertullian quotes its words as those of a companion of the Apostles—Barnabas in his view—'ex redundantia,' as a work of supererogation; and alleges that it was more widely accepted in the Churches than the Shepherd of Hermas—a form of praise which, with Tertullian, is not far removed from censure.[1] Further, though Marcion rejected this Epistle, Tertullian does not count this among his many offences. In the next generation Cyprian does not quote the Hebrews, and, as he lays stress on St. Paul's having written to *seven* churches, he by implication rejects it. A century later the Epistle is omitted in the African list of Books preserved in the Cheltenhem MS.[2] Lastly, towards the end of the fourth century Jerome (*Ep.* cxxix. 3) and Augustine (*De Peccatorum Mer.* i. 27) both accepted the Epistle as Canonical in reliance on the authority of the Eastern Churches, the former expressly noting that "the custom of the Latins does not receive it among the Canonical Scriptures," and balancing this rejection of the Hebrews by Western Churches against the rejection of the Apocalypse by 'the Churches of the Greeks.'

To sum up, the West, making apostolic authorship the criterion of canonicity, refused to accept the Epistle to the Hebrews. The East recognized the apostolic character of the Epistle and accounted it as

[1] Tert. *de Pudicitia* 20. Possibly the phrase 'receptior apud ecclesias' means 'more worthy to be accepted in the Churches' rather than 'more widely in the Churches.'

[2] The MS. containing this list was discovered in 1885 by Professor Mommsen in the Phillipps Collection at Cheltenham; hence it is commonly called the Cheltenham List. The time when the list was made was shortly after 350 A.D.

Scripture, in earlier days maintaining that in some secondary sense it was the work of St. Paul, and in later times asserting without qualification the Pauline authorship. The Eastern view was accepted by Jerome and Augustine, and the inclusion of the Epistle in the Latin Vulgate closed the question in the West.

(2) THE APOCALYPSE.—At the end of the second century the Apocalypse was widely accepted—by Hippolytus at Rome (with whom we may connect the Muratorian Canon), by Tertullian at Carthage, by Clement at Alexandria, by Irenaeus in South Gaul. The evidence of Irenaeus is of special importance. The passage (v. 30) in which Irenaeus deals with the Apocalypse presents perhaps the earliest discussion of a variation of reading in the New Testament. In place of 666, the number of the Beast (Apoc. xiii. 18), some in the time of Irenaeus read 616. Irenaeus maintains the reading 666 on three grounds. (α) He appeals, as we should say, to 'documentary evidence.' "That number," he says, "is found in all the good and ancient copies." (β) He appeals to oral tradition. "Those who had seen John face to face used to give their testimony to it." (γ) He appeals, to use our modern phrase, to 'intrinsic probability.' "Reason teaches us" that it is appropriate that the same number should repeat itself in the hundreds, the tens, and as the unit. You will observe that the mention of "the good and ancient

copies" implies both wide circulation and antiquity. The occurrence also of variations of reading in different copies of a Book is an evidence of age. Some ten years earlier than Irenaeus we know that the Apocalypse was used by Theophilus at Antioch (Eus. *H.E.* iv. 24), and by Melito at Sardis; the latter indeed made it the subject of a treatise (Eus. *H.E.* iv. 26). Even more important is the evidence of Justin Martyr about the middle of the century. The Apocalypse is the only Book of the New Testament whose author Justin mentions by name. "Among us," he says (*Dial.* 81; comp. Eus. *H.E.* iv. 18. 8), "a certain man whose name was John, one of the Apostles of the Christ, in an apocalypse vouchsafed to him, prophesied that those who believe our Christ will pass a thousand years in Jerusalem, and that after this there will be the general and (in a word) the eternal resurrection of all men, and the judgment." Thus in the second century the evidence for the acceptance of the Apocalypse as an Apostolic writing, the work of St. John, is remarkably varied, strong, and early. But when from the second we turn to the third century we become aware of discordant notes.

A certain sect, called from its founder the Montanists, though they were guilty of no formal heresy, broke away from the Catholic Church mainly on certain questions of discipline. They were the

Puritans of the early Church. They were characterized by two opinions. On the one hand they exaggerated and distorted the doctrine of the Paraclete (the Holy Ghost, the Comforter), in that they insisted that the Spirit made revelations to members of their body, and that these revelations were binding on the whole number of the Faithful. On the other hand, they dwelt with unusual vigour on the conception of the millennium kingdom—Christ's reign on earth for a thousand years. The former of these views was based on the teaching of St. John's Gospel, the latter on the symbolism of the Apocalypse. Hence some who opposed their characteristic doctrines, strove to cut at the root of the mischief by calling in question the Gospel and the Apocalypse of St. John. Caius, a presbyter, early in the third century, in a disputation which he held at Rome with Proclus, a Montanist leader, appears absurdly enough to have ascribed the Apocalypse to Cerinthus, a contemporary of St. John, who denied the true humanity of Christ (Eus. *H.E.* iii. 28). Again, a certain nebulous sect, whom Epiphanius (*Haer.* li.) nicknamed the Alogi (the irrational ones[1]), went a step further and rejected

[1] The name Alogi refers both to their supposed character—those who were without reason (*logos*); and to the fact that in rejecting St. John's Gospel they rejected the doctrine of the Word (*Logos*). They are also probably alluded to in Irenaeus iii. 11. 9.

both the Gospel and the Apocalypse, affirming that they were the work not of the Apostle but of the heresiarch, Cerinthus. Thus, though no historical evidence was alleged against the Apocalypse, yet because of the extravagances of those who misused its imagery it fell into discredit. A more cautious and reverent criticism meets us in some fragments, preserved by Eusebius (*H.E.* vii. 25), of a letter of Dionysius, a great bishop of Alexandria about the year 260. Dionysius, with the precision of a scholar, notes the differences in general character, in literary style, and in vocabulary which separate the Fourth Gospel and the Apocalypse. The two books cannot, he argues, be the work of the same writer. John the Apostle was the author of the Gospel. That the writer of the Apocalypse was 'a holy and inspired man' Dionysius admits, and that his name was John; but he cannot have been the same John who wrote the Gospel. The fragment illustrates in a remarkable degree the reverent freedom with which the question of the authorship of a Scriptural Book was discussed in the third century, and the critical and literary insight which was brought to bear on such problems. In the fourth century we find a remarkable division of opinion and practice. Turning to the Eastern (Greek) Church, we note that the Apocalypse was included in some lists of Books (*e.g.* that of Athanasius), that it was omitted in others (*e.g.* that of Cyril of Jerusalem), that it was included in others with an expression of doubt (*e.g.* that of Eusebius and that of Amphilochius, Bishop of Iconium). It is a noteworthy fact that Chrysostom, presbyter of Antioch and afterwards Archbishop of Constantinople, though it is clear that he was acquainted with it, yet, in all his voluminous works, abstains from any appeal to the Apocalypse as a doctrinal authority. "Sometimes," in writers of this century, to quote some unpublished words of Dr. Hort, "but rarely, one comes across a shy quotation. It was probably accepted as a matter of form, but passed over as a matter of practice."

In the West, on the other hand, the Apocalypse was generally accepted. "We receive them both," wrote Jerome (*Ep.* cxxix. 3, referring to the Apocalypse and the Epistle to the Hebrews), "not following the custom of our own time, but the authority of ancient writers, who often adduce quotations from them, as from Canonical and Ecclesiastical Books."

How then are we to account for this remarkable divergence between the earliest and later times, between the estimate of the Book in the second century and that of the fourth? It was probably due partly to the cause to which I have already alluded—the condemnation of millenarian views, which were based, or were supposed to be based, on the teaching of the Book; partly to the suspicion under which the Apocalyptic literature, of which the so-called Apocalypse of Peter is a conspicuous example, fell in the fourth century. But whatever doubts were current in later times as to its fitness for popular use or as to its Apostolic authority it is important to remember that in the second century, when the traditions of the Apostolic age were still living, it was held in high estimation. It was accepted by Melito and Irenaeus, the pupils of those teachers in Asia Minor who had themselves been the pupils of St. John.

(3) THE CATHOLIC EPISTLES.—The collection of Catholic Epistles may be compared with that in the Hebrew Bible called the כתובים (the Writings).[1] Both collections were formed latest in their respective Canons. Both included Books about which there had been doubt. Both were to some extent miscellaneous; for in the New Testament Canon the two shorter Epistles of St. John were not, properly speaking, Catholic (General) Epistles.

In the early Syriac Church it appears that no Catholic Epistle was accepted. "The Law and the Prophets and the Gospel," to quote an important

---

[1] The Hebrew Bible is arranged as follows: (1) The Law; (2) The Former Prophets (Joshua, Judges, 1, 2 Samuel, 1, 2 Kings); (3) The Later Prophets; (4) The Writings (Psalms, Proverbs, Job, Song of Solomon, Ruth, Lamentations, Ecclesiastes, Esther, Daniel, Ezra, Nehemiah, 1, 2 Chronicles).

passage from an ancient Syriac work called *The Doctrine of Addai* (p. 44, ed. Phillips), "which ye read every day before the people, and the Epistles of St. Paul, which Simon Peter sent us from the city of Rome, and the Acts of the twelve Apostles, which John, the son of Zebedee, sent us from Ephesus, these Books read ye in the Churches of Christ, and with these read not any others, as there is not any other in which the truth which ye hold is written, except these Books."

In the growth of the collection of the Catholic Epistles we may trace three stages.

(*a*) The nucleus of the collection consisted of the First Epistle of St. Peter and the First Epistle of St. John. Of the "authority" of these two Epistles, to use the words of the sixth article, "was never any doubt in the Church."

(*b*) The Collection of Three Epistles.—To these two Epistles (1 Peter, 1 John) that of St. James was added. This collection represented the teaching of the three Apostles of the Circumcision, and it was obviously complementary to the collection of Pauline Epistles. The fact that the Epistle of St. James commonly held the first place among the Catholic Epistles (cf. Eus. *H.E.* ii. 23. 25) points to the conclusion that this collection of three Epistles had its origin in Syria, perhaps in Jerusalem. These three Epistles formed the Canon of the

Catholic Epistles in the great Syriac version of the New Testament. They alone were accepted in the neighbouring Church of Antioch—that Church of which John Chrysostom is the most famous representative. Amphilochius, Bishop of Iconium about 380 A.D., in his list of Books, speaks of some persons who say that "three only [of the Catholic Epistles] ought to be received—one of James, one of Peter, and one of John."

Of the Epistle of St. James it may be briefly said that in the East, if it was not very extensively used, no doubts were expressed as to its authority. It was in the West that its position was questioned. At Carthage Tertullian's supposed allusions to its language are very doubtful; Cyprian, from whose quotations a large part of the New Testament could be re-written, never uses it; a century later it is omitted in the 'Cheltenham' list of New Testament Books. At Rome, as the silence of the Muratorian Fragment shews, it was ignored. There is no evidence that Irenaeus in South Gaul was acquainted with it. On the other hand, traces of its language are found in Clement of Rome, in the Teaching of the Twelve Apostles, and in the Shepherd of Hermas. The last-named writer indeed had clearly a special reverence for it, and knew it by heart. It is probable that, owing to the original circumstances of its destination (it is addressed to the Jewish Dispersion), and to its peculiar character (though it is full of echoes of Christ's teaching, it hardly mentions His name, and never alludes to His death or resurrection), it had a limited circulation, epecially in the West; and, as it touched Christian doctrine at but few points and had no bearing on the theological controversies of the early centuries, it attracted little attention. It was probably the influence of the Churches of Syria and of the further East which gained for it a place in the Canon.

(*c*) The Collection of Seven Epistles.—The first mention of seven Catholic Epistles is found in a passage of Eusebius (*H.E.* ii. 23. 25). There were obvious reasons why, as there were four Epistles bearing Apostolic names and therefore challenging a place in the Canon, the collection of Catholic Epistles should be extended from three to seven. Seven is the sacred number of perfection. Moreover, the increase to seven created an analogy between the Catholic Epistles and on the one hand the Apocalypse, addressed to the seven Churches of Asia Minor, and on the other hand the collection of Pauline Epistles. For St. Paul, as it used often to be said, wrote to seven Churches; or, if the Epistle to the Hebrews be included among his writings, then his Epistles are twice seven in number. There is some evidence to shew that this full collection of seven Catholic Epistles either originated at, or was first established in, the Church of Jerusalem.

The Epistles of St. Jude and the Second Epistle of St. Peter[1] were both included, you will remember, among the books which Eusebius calls 'disputed'; and both, but especially the latter, present to the student of the New Testament problems of peculiar difficulty.

As to the Epistle of St. Jude, little or no stress can be laid on supposed coincidences with this Epistle in the writings of the second century. But there is clear evidence that at the meeting point of the second and third centuries it was accepted as authoritative in the Churches of the countries round the Mediterranean, at Alexandria, at Carthage, at Rome. In the third century, however, doubts were expressed about its apostolic authority, based on the contents of the Epistle itself. At Alexandria Origen, if in one passage (*in Matt.* tom. x. 17) he commends it as "full of strong words of heavenly grace, though it be but a few lines in length," yet in another hints at misgivings as to its reception: "If any one should adduce the Epistle of Jude" (*ib.* xvii. 30). At Carthage, though it was used by Tertullian, yet it is ignored in the writings of Cyprian and in the African list of New Testament Books of a century later. It

[1] For a fuller discussion of these two Epistles I may be allowed to refer to my articles on them in Hastings' *Dictionary of the Bible.*

apparently was not accepted in the great Biblical School of Antioch. The reason of these suspicions is not far to seek. Didymus, the blind head of the Catechetical School of Alexandria about 390, informs us that the Epistle was questioned by some on account of the strange reference in it to the dispute of the Archangel with the devil about the body of Moses, a reference which was doubtless derived from an apocryphal Book called the *Assumption of Moses.* Further, we learn from Jerome that it was rejected 'by many' because it quoted from the Book of Enoch. Here then, as in the case of the Apocalypse, we have a contrast between earlier and later opinion. From the beginning of the third century, when there was a growing tendency in view of the Gnostic controversies to regard all apocryphal writings with suspicion, the use of such writings in this Epistle became a bar to its recognition as an authoritative apostolic document. On the other hand, considering the brevity of the Epistle and its special character, it had received by the beginning of the third century a remarkably wide acceptance in the Church. This early acceptance, it will be observed, may well embody a tradition handed down from the Apostolic age.

The Second Epistle of Peter must be said to stand apart from the other Books of the New Testament in regard to the insufficiency of its external support.

With the internal characteristics of the Book we do not concern ourselves to-day.

In the extant literature of the second century there seems to be no trace of the influence of this Epistle, no reminiscence of its thought or language. This lack of evidence is all the more striking, because the style of the Epistle is so remarkable that its phrases, if known, could hardly fail to be remembered; and, if regarded as apostolic, to be appealed to. The Epistle would have been a controversial armoury for the assailants of the Gnostics. Had he known it and regarded it as authoritative, it could not but have been used, as the First and Second Epistles of St. John are used, by Irenaeus. The earliest *certain* reference to the Epistle is contained in the words of Origen (*ap.* Eus. *H.E.* vi. 25. 8), "Peter has left one Epistle, which is acknowledged, and perhaps also a second; for it is doubted." It is, however, probable that the Epistle was known at Alexandria shortly before the time of Origen. There are reasons for thinking that Clement of Alexandria commented on 2 Peter; but he also, as we learn from Eusebius (*H.E.* vi. 14. 1), commented on the so-called *Apocalypse of Peter*; and the evidence points to the conclusion that he regarded the Epistle in question as the companion of the *Apocalypse of Peter* rather than of the First Epistle of that Apostle.

During the third century the Epistle, it is clear,

gained acceptance in certain churches. We find traces of it in the works of Hippolytus of Rome, in two writers of Asia Minor (Firmilian of Caesarea in Cappadocia and Methodius of Patara). Fragments of an old Latin translation of the Epistle are extant, but the translation belongs to the later Italian type of text. It is contained in the two great Egyptian versions, the date of which however is uncertain.

By the time when Eusebius wrote in the fourth century the recognition of seven Catholic Epistles (at least in the Churches which he knew best) had become usual. The Second Epistle of Peter was accepted at Jerusalem, as Cyril's list shews. But it had no place in the Canon of the Syriac-speaking Churches nor in that of the Greek school of Antioch. In Asia Minor, if 2 Peter is included in the list of Gregory Nazianzen, yet neither he nor Gregory of Nyssa nor Basil the Great appears to quote it or to refer to it. Those teachers, whose knowledge of Christian literature prior to their days was widest, were conscious how little support the Epistle had in early writers. Its reception was probably due to the popular voice. This is what we infer from the words of Eusebius (*H.E.* iii. 3), which also tell us of his own inability to accept it: "As to the current Second Epistle [of Peter], we have learned (παρειλήφαμεν) that it is not canonical:

yet since it seemed useful to many, it was studied along with the other Scriptures. . . . Of the writings which bear the name of Peter I recognize one single Epistle as genuine and acknowledged by the elders of old time. When once it "was studied with the other Scriptures," it could not fail to attach itself to the undisputed Epistle of Peter; for it proclaimed itself (iii. 1) a 'Second Epistle' of that Apostle. Thus the Epistle was ready, when the collection of Catholic Epistles was extended to seven, to take its place beside that Epistle of St. Peter which had been accepted from the first.

We have now traced in outline the history of the selection of single Books and of the formation of the various groups of Books. How was the final result attained? A different issue, humanly speaking, would not have been an unnatural one. The Apocalypse might well have been excluded from the Canon of the New Testament in deference to the scruples of those who questioned the apostolicity of its teaching. It would not have been surprising if the smaller group of Catholic Epistles had been accepted, and not the larger one. The acknowledgment of the full Canon of the New Testament is probably due to two influences, the workings of which synchronized.

We turn first to the Greek Churches of the East. Among these Churches Constantinople was in the fourth century a centre of rapidly increasing importance. It was the 'New Rome.' The Church of Constantinople, in many ways the daughter of the Church of Antioch, did not inherit the doubts of Antioch as to the full Canon of the New Testament. Constantinople was the centre of those imperial influences, which played so great a part in matters ecclesiastical and religious. The preparation which Constantine entrusted to Eusebius of 'fifty copies of the Divine Scriptures' for use in the new capital (Eus. *v. c.* iv. 36) had important results. It was not unnatural that these copies should contain all the Books of the New Testament which had gained general recognition. A quasi-official standard was thus set up; and the distinction, so clearly drawn, as we have seen, in the writings of Eusebius himself, between 'acknowledged' and 'disputed' Books, soon became little more than a matter of antiquarian interest.

In Western Christendom the decisive influences were those of Jerome and of Augustine. The latter, though not insensible of the effect on the authority or the prestige of a Book caused by its rejection in some quarters (*de Doct. Christ.* ii. 12, 13), yet in practice appealed, without distinction, to all the Books of our New Testament. Jerome, as a student of earlier Church writers, Greek and Latin, was acquainted with the doubts of scholars as to certain Books, but for the purposes of instruction and edification he puts these all on one side, and uses all the Books which make up our New Testament without any sign of differentiating between them. This view, which doubtless represents that of the Church of Rome, found expression in the Canon of the Vulgate. The publication of the Vulgate closed the question in the West. The New Testament Canon of the Syriac-speaking people still remained more restricted in its range. But the verdict of the Greek and the verdict of the Latin Churches, which made themselves felt about the same time, fixed the limits of the New Testament, which has been the 'divine library' of Christendom from the end of the fourth century to the present day.

I bring this lecture to a close with three brief observations.

(1) The Canon of the New Testament, as we have seen, was a gradual growth, not the creation of any formal enactment. As we look back over the history as a whole, we can discern how the Providence of God in the earliest times guarded the Apostolic writings, and preserved them from countless possibilities of destruction; and in later times moulded the apparently fortuitous and casual course

of events, so that, as the final result, the Canon included the full sum of Apostolic teaching—the ethical teaching of St. James, for example, as well as the spiritual witness of St. John.

(2) We recognize that the Books of the New Testament do not all stand on the same level of certainty and authority. No doubt the popular view is that the New Testament is a single Book, and that there is no difference between its constituent parts. The study of the history of the growth of the Canon does not support this opinion. It is a serious confusion if we regard the Gospel of St. John as possessing no greater attestation than the Second Epistle of St. Peter. In the Canon of the New Testament there is the clear noon of certitude and the twilight of ambiguity. Christ gave to His Church not a charter of infallibility, but the sure promise of a guiding Spirit.

(3) We thankfully acknowledge the unique and sure position of those Apostolic writings which are the title-deeds of our Christian faith and life—the Gospels, the Acts, the Epistles of St. Paul, the two great Epistles of St. Peter and St. John. The Christian society from the first days recognized and treasured these Books as the work and the abiding witness of the Apostles, and as such handed them on as the Sacred Scriptures of the New Covenant to all future generations of Christian men.

The Dates of the New Testament Books.

DURING the present course of lectures you have had put before you an account of the transmission of the New Testament to our own time, and of the process by which a New Testament Canon was created. Both lines of investigation trace the history of the books, to which we owe our knowledge of the origin and contents of the Christian Revelation back to a very early period. Following on these it is my duty to try and put before you the evidence which enables us to determine within certain limits the date at which these books were written. To any one who is in the least acquainted with the subject this will seem a bold thing to attempt within the limits of a single lecture. He will know that volumes have been written about each separate book. But there is sometimes an advantage in attempting a comprehensive view, in emphasising the essential points, and in trying to dissociate from the cloud of conjectures and theories which surround the subject such facts as may lay some claim to certainty. The fundamental question is this: There is a traditional view, according to which the books of the New Testament are the work of Apostolic or subapostolic authors, and were written at different dates during the second half of the first century. There is, on the other hand, an immense amount of critical work, which has set itself to prove that all, or the greater number, or at any rate some of these books were the product of the Christian imagination of the second century. We have not to attempt to-day to discuss the exact date of each writing, but to decide which of these views is correct or most nearly correct.

I.

I will begin with certain general considerations, and, in order to get a substantial basis of external evidence, I will ask you to look at the Christian remains of the beginning of the second century. We possess five short writings, the claim of which to be written not later than the first quarter of that century may be considered to have been made good. Of course I do not mean that no one disputes it, but whether one looks at the weight of the argument by which it is supported, or at the wide acceptance which they have received, one may reasonably hold that this conclusion has been accepted by scholarship. At any rate the dates which I am going to give you are those which have been adopted by Dr. Abbott in his article on the Gospels in the *Encyclopaedia Biblica*, and as he is one of the ablest representatives in England of the views which I believe to be incorrect, it is convenient to have a starting point on which we are agreed.

The documents in question are :

(1) A letter written by the Roman Church to the Church of Corinth, generally held to be the work of a certain Clement, and called the *First Epistle of Clement*. Its date is probably about 96 A.D.

(2) *Seven Letters of Ignatius*, Bishop of Antioch, to certain churches in the province of Asia, and to the Church of Rome about the year 110 A.D.

(3) A short *Letter of Polycarp*, Bishop of Smyrna, written about the same time.

(4) A curious document, perhaps a sermon, called the *Epistle of Barnabas*, written not later than 125 A.D., and perhaps shortly after 70 A.D.

(5) The recently discovered treatise called the *Didache* or *Teaching of the Twelve Apostles*, written, according to Abbott, between 80

A.D. and 110 A.D. This is the only document for which such an early date, although probable, has not, in my opinion, been completely proved. For it is composite in character; and although some portions are not only early, but very early, the latest date at which additions or interpolations may have been made cannot be conclusively settled.

Before proceeding to ask what evidence these writings give, I will ask you to notice two or three further points. They are, in the first place, exceedingly short. The whole bulk only occupies in English about 100 octavo pages, and might be read in two or three hours. Then they represent very widely different areas—Rome, Asia, Syria, probably Palestine and Egypt. And then, thirdly, they were written at a time when the Christian Scriptures were normally at any rate the Old Testament writings. This is of course itself a proof of their early age. They were written by men who owed their Christianity to the oral teaching of the Apostles themselves and their immediate followers, and hence the use of the New Testament books is mainly incidental. When these facts are remembered it will be seen how very important and how strong the evidence, which we shall proceed to examine, really is.

It is of three kinds. There is first of all their witness to the subject matter of the New Testament, to the Christian Faith and the Gospel History. There is, secondly, their witness to the different types of teaching given in the New Testament. And then, thirdly, there is their testimony to the actual words and language of the books which we possess.

(1) The Apostolic Fathers taught and preached just the same gospel that we now read in the New Testament, *i.e.* the same teaching about the life of Christ, about the doctrinal significance of that life, and the moral obligations of Christianity.

Let me take an instance from Ignatius: "I give glory to Jesus Christ, the God who bestowed such wisdom upon you; for I have perceived that ye are established in faith immoveable, being as it were nailed to the Cross of the Lord Jesus Christ, in flesh and in spirit, and firmly grounded in love in the blood of Christ, fully persuaded as touching our Lord that he is truly of the race of David according to the flesh, but Son of God by the Divine will and power, truly born of a virgin and baptized by John that *all righteousness might be fulfilled* by Him, truly nailed up in the flesh for our sakes under Pontius Pilate and Herod the tetrarch (of which fruit are we—that is of His most blessed passion); that *He might set up an ensign* unto all the ages through His resurrection, for His saints and faithful people, whether among

Jews or among Gentiles, in the body of His Church. For He suffered all these things for our sakes ; and He suffered truly as also He raised Himself truly."[1]

Now here we have substantially the Gospel as we know it, and it must, I think, be perfectly evident that the writer of this passage, if he had not the same gospels as we have, had documents which told exactly the same message. Moreover, every characteristic of style and reflection shows that this passage is later than the Gospel story.

Bishop Westcott in his *History of the Canon* has summed up for us the knowledge of the Gospel shown in the Apostolic Fathers.

"The 'Gospel' which the Fathers announce includes all the articles of the ancient Creeds. Christ, we read, our God, the Word, the Lord and Creator of the World, who was with the Father before time began, humbled Himself and came down from heaven, and was manifested in the flesh, and was born of the Virgin Mary, of the race of David according to the flesh ; and a star of exceeding brightness appeared at His birth. Afterwards He was baptized by John, *to fulfil all righteousness* ; and then, speaking His Father's message, He invited not the righteous, but sinners, to come to Him. Perfume was poured *over His head*, an emblem of the immortality which He breathed on the Church. At length, under

[1] Ignatius, *Smyrn.* I. (Lightfoot's translation).

Herod and Pontius Pilate, He was crucified, and vinegar and gall were offered Him to drink. But on the first day of the week He rose from the dead, the first fruits of the grave; and many prophets were raised by Him for whom they had waited. After His resurrection He ate with His disciples and showed them that He was not an incorporeal spirit. And He ascended into heaven and sat down on the right hand of the Father, and thence he shall come to judge the quick and the dead."[1]

(2) But this indebtedness to Apostolic teaching is still more marked. There are, apart from the Gospel narratives, five main types of teaching in the New Testament. That of St. Paul, of St. James, of the Epistle to the Hebrews, of St. Peter, and St. John. Of these five types four are presupposed and harmonized in the Epistle of Clement, and the fifth, that of St. John has influenced the Epistles of St. Ignatius. Clement co-ordinates St. Peter and St. Paul. He combines their favourite expressions. He is largely indebted to the Epistle to the Hebrews. He states the doctrine of justification in all its antithetical fulness, combining the views and the instances of St. James and St. Paul.

"The theory of justification," writes Bishop Westcott, "is stated in its antithetical fulness. The

---

[1] *A History of the Canon of the New Testament*, by Brooke Foss Westcott, p. 53, Edn. 5, 1881.

same examples are used as in the Canonical Epistles, and the teaching of St. Paul and St. James is coincidentally affirmed. 'Through faith and hospitality a son was given to Abraham in old age, and by obedience he offered him a sacrifice to God.' 'Through faith and hospitality Rahab was saved.' 'We are not justified by ourselves . . . nor by works which we have wrought in holiness of heart, but by our faith, by which Almighty God justified all from the beginning of the world.' Shortly afterwards Clement adds in the Spirit of St. James, 'Let us then work from our whole heart the work of righteousness.' And the same tenor of thought reappears in the continual reference to the fear of God as instrumental in the accomplishment of these good works."[1]

If we pass to Ignatius, while it is on the teaching of St. Paul that his thoughts are built up—'The image of St. Paul is stamped alike upon their language and doctrine'—he is also acquainted with and influenced by the mode of thought peculiar to St. John.

"Love is 'the stamp of the Christian.' 'Faith is the beginning, and love the end of life.' 'Faith is our guide upward, but love is the road that leads to God.' 'The Word is the manifestation of God,' 'the door by which we come to the Father,' 'and without Him we have not the principle of true life.' 'The Spirit is not led astray, as being from God.

[1] Westcott, *op. cit.* p. 25.

For it knoweth whence it cometh and whither it goeth and telleth that which is hidden.' The true meat of the Christian is the 'bread of God, the bread of heaven, the bread of life, which is the flesh of Jesus Christ,' and his drink is 'Christ's blood, which is love incorruptible.' He has no love of this life; 'his love has been crucified, and he has in him no burning passion for the world, but living water, speaking within him, and bidding him come to his Father.' Meanwhile his enemy is the enemy of his Master, even the 'ruler of this age.'"[1]

Now we may state the problem in this way. Here are a series of writers of the sub-apostolic Age, all of them professing to give the teaching of the Apostles. They write, allowing for differences of style and method of thought, just as an orthodox Christian might at the present day with the New Testament before him. They have their individual peculiarities. Some are more, some less original. But their doctrine and theological teaching are the same. Where did they get it from? The natural answer is, from the books of the New Testament which we now possess, and from which we can get the same teaching. They had, it is true, the advantage of remembering some oral tradition, but oral tradition would have confined them to one or two lines of thought. With these writers Christianity

[1] Westcott, *op. cit.* p. 35.

has already become Catholic. Different strains of teaching are combined. If we had no New Testament, we should have to assume one to explain the phenomena of their writings, and if they did not use the books which we still possess they must have had others with the same contents and the same teaching.

(3) But, thirdly, our case is stronger still. There are in the writings of the Apostolic Fathers a large number of resemblances in language to almost all the books of the New Testament. In some cases the quotations are full, in others slight ; in some they are more exact than in others, but they extend over the whole range of the New Testament, with the exception of three or four of the smaller books.[1] In some cases the evidence is far less full than in others. I am only now asking you to look at it as a whole, and I would put it before you as a result of the examination of the Apostolic Fathers, that they imply something very like our New Testament, that the natural, I will not say certain, deduction from this line of investigation is that the books of the New Testament were mainly written in the

---

[1] The strength and value of this evidence may to some extent be recognized by the list of quotations given in the Appendix, in which passages from the Apostolic Fathers are placed side by side with verses of the New Testament, to which the writers appeared to be indebted.

first century, and recognized in the Christian Churches as authoritative, I will not say canonical, at the beginning of the second century. May I add that if you wish to understand the early history of Christianity, a careful study of the Apostolic Fathers, which are all perfectly accessible in the excellent translations and editions of Bishop Lightfoot, will be far more profitable than pages of magazine articles and popular pamphlets, which are often singularly ignorant.

While we are still considering the New Testament generally, I should like to mention two further arguments which are making careful enquirers feel more and more clearly that the evidence requires them to trace back the writings of the New Testament into the first century. The one is the history of the Canon, the other the result of New Testament criticism. By the middle of the second century (if not earlier) our Gospels were in all probability collected together as one book, and that in a text which had already begun to be corrupted. I will quote in support of this some remarks of von Dobschütz in a review of Mr. Burkitt's *Two Lectures on the Gospels* in the *Theologische Literaturzeitung*, a leading German review: "Burkitt's results lie exactly in the line of the observations, which in every direction—and not merely in Textual criticism—have forced themselves upon me as the result of the most recent research. We are continually being forced onward right to the very beginnings and origins. We have learnt to place the beginnings of text corruption, and also of the misinterpretation of the Gospels, not in the fourth century, not even in the second century, but already in the first."[1] This line of argument is somewhat subtle, and requires a certain amount of special knowledge to appreciate, but it is probably more certain than many more obvious forms of evidence.

II.

We will pass now from the general question to the different groups of books, and will begin with the thirteen Epistles of St. Paul. On both external and internal grounds these can be dated with more certainty than perhaps any other books of the New Testament, and they need not detain us long. Their use by the Apostolic Fathers is clear and undoubted. There are quotations from all of them, with the exception of the Epistle to Philemon. Of certain books they are slight and not such as stress could be laid on if they were alone. Of the more important, of Romans, of I. Corinthians, and Ephesians, the use is large. It is difficult to avoid believing that Polycarp had a collection of the Epistles including the Pastorals. Of the question of style and doctrine

[1] *Theologische Literaturzeitung*, 1902, 1. p. 21

I need only speak shortly, as Dr. Sanday has already treated that subject. They divide internally into four groups corresponding to four periods in St. Paul's life. They have a remarkable and distinct resemblance both in teaching and style, and also certain differences which correspond exactly to these different chronological divisions. They reveal in all cases a marked and striking personality, and imply rather than narrate a series of circumstances which fit into the narrative as we possess it in the Acts of the Apostles. I am not going now to discuss the exact date to which each can be assigned, that would necessarily lead us to a number of minute and often doubtful points, which would be irrelevant to our present purpose. I will give you the approximate date for each group :

I. Epistles of the Second Missionary Journey, I. and II. Thessalonians, 48-51 A.D.

II. Epistles of the Third Missionary Journey, Galatians, I. and II. Corinthians, Romans, 50-58 A.D.

III. Epistles of the Captivity, 57-61 A.D.

IV. The Pastoral Epistles, 58-64 A.D.[1]

With regard to these, I hardly think it necessary to apologize for treating them as genuine, with the exception perhaps of the Pastoral Epistles. On these I would say :

(i.) The great difficulty to me has always been the

[1] These dates represent the outside limits according to different systems of chronology.

question of the release and second imprisonment; it was difficult to find room for them before the Neronian persecutions in 64. But a series of chronological investigations, made by Mr. Turner in England and Professor Harnack in Germany, have tended to throw the dates of St. Paul's life further back. They depend upon the date at which Festus succeeded Felix, which is now put in 55/56 instead of as late as 60 or 61. This leaves ample room in St. Paul's life for the later activity implied by the Pastoral Epistles.

(ii.) The differences of style and subject matter are hardly greater than between other groups of the Pauline Epistles, and may be quite sufficiently accounted for by the later date and the different style and character of the writings.

(iii.) The external evidence for the letters is very good.

(iv.) The argument against their genuineness, based on the supposed developed ecclesiastical conditions, is a very precarious one, and we have really no knowledge which enables us to condemn a document on such grounds. It is an argument of an *a priori* character and often means arguing in a circle. But I should be inclined to say that the Pastoral Epistles represent an early and primitive type of organization, very much earlier than that of the Ignatius letters, and that they must be put certainly one generation earlier than the latter. They represent much the same stage as the Acts of the Apostles.

(v.) Even those who deny their genuineness, for the most part consider that there is a primitive nucleus, which they date to these closing years of St. Paul's life. If that is once admitted to be possible, every solid argument against their genuineness vanishes.[1]

III.

It will be convenient to take next the Epistle to the Hebrews, both because the problem that it presents is for us a fairly simple one, and because it naturally, if incorrectly, groups itself with the Epistles of St. Paul. Amongst much that is obscure there are two things fairly certain—one, that it was not and could not have been written by St. Paul; the other, that it must have been written before the close of the first century. There is no book the early date of which is better attested. When we come to ask further questions we soon reach the uncertain—

[1] It is difficult to know whether it is necessary to treat seriously the opinions put forward by von Manen, and accessible for English readers in an article by himself in the *Encyclopaedia Biblica*, III. 3620-3638: "With respect to the Canonical Epistles the later criticism . . . has learned to recognize that they are none of them by Paul." These views have attained no assent outside his own circle, and are not supported by any arguments which need refutation.

"Who wrote it?" as Origen says, "God only knows." Where it was written, to whom it was written are equally doubtful. Harnack has recently startled us by suggesting that it was a woman that wrote it. There is one question, however, which it may be worth attempting to answer—Was it written before or after the destruction of Jerusalem? On this point opinion may reasonably be divided. My own opinion has varied somewhat, but I feel that the preponderating evidence is in favour of the earlier date. We cannot, I think, lay stress on the fact that the rites of the Jewish temple are spoken of in the present tense. That might be an ordinary historic present. But we can, I think, say perfectly reasonably that it would be astonishing that such an Epistle could be written after the destruction of the Temple without any reference to that event. But still more striking, I think, is the aim of the Epistle. The difficulty of those who are addressed is the feeling of being cut off from the rites of the Temple and the Jewish ordinances. Surely if the writer was able to point to the judgment of God in their discontinuance his argument would hardly have been necessary. But this remains a matter of opinion. To some the Epistle seems to be directed to the situation caused by the destruction of Jerusalem. While inclined personally to date the Epistle between the years

65 and 70, reasonable criticism must allow the margin 65-90.

IV.

We now pass to a section of the New Testament where there is wider room for controversy, viz., the Synoptic Gospels and the Acts of the Apostles. I will begin with the writings ascribed to St. Luke, because here, as has been generally recognized, is a fixed point. There can be no doubt that the third Gospel and the Acts of the Apostles were written by the same person; they clearly claim to be, and there is a marked and striking unity of style. They are the most literary, the most carefully composed, the most Hellenic of all the writings of the New Testament. But, further, the writer must have been a companion of St. Paul. There are, as you know well, certain sections in the Acts of the Apostles in which the narrative passes into the first person plural, and no explanation of the existence of these sections is satisfactory, except that which makes them the work of the author of the book writing naturally in the first person plural, because he was at that point a companion of St. Paul. It might be argued (as it has been) that here we have extracts from a diary —but the style is identical in these sections with that of the rest of the book; or that the first person was introduced for the sake of *vraisemblance*, but in that case how do we account for the fact that just in these sections the narrative in its fulness of detail, in its accuracy, its vividness, and knowledge bears all the marks of being the work of one eye-witness? I feel personally quite confident of the correctness of the conclusion, which is that of Ramsay, of Blass, of Renan, beside orthodox writers, in fact of all but certain extreme writers on the other side, that these two books were written by a companion of St. Paul. The earliest date for the Acts must be after the close of the two years mentioned in the concluding chapter, *i.e.* about the year 60; the latest date will be 85–90. The Gospel of St. Luke must be earlier, but not necessarily very much earlier than the Acts. The only strong argument for a long interval between the composition of the two books would be certain differences of vocabulary between them, but that may, I think, be discounted by the very different subject-matter of the two writings, and by the fact that certainly the Gospels, and in part perhaps the Acts, have their style very largely influenced by the sources used by the writer.

Have we any possibility of dating them more exactly? There are two more or less conflicting arguments:

(1) Many writers have assumed that the somewhat abrupt ending of the Acts, leaving St. Paul preaching at Rome, arose from the fact that the book was written

and finished during these two years. But this is not an argument on which any real stress can be laid, since, as a matter of fact, the Acts ends where it does because the writer has brought St. Paul to Rome, and thus fulfilled his purpose of describing the spread of Christianity to the uttermost parts of the world.

(2) An argument for a later date of the Gospel is found in a comparison of Luke xxi. 20, with Matt. xxiv. 15, Mark xiii. 14, where the words, "When ye see the abomination of desolation standing where it ought not," seem to be interpreted by St. Luke as "When you see Jerusalem compassed with armies." It has been held to imply that St. Luke was interpreting the prophecy by the event, and that therefore the Gospel was written after the Fall of Jerusalem. But here again no decisive conclusion can be drawn. The phrase in St. Matthew and St. Mark would be obscure and unmeaning to a Gentile reader, and St. Luke may well have interpreted it in a natural way, even before the event had happened, or when it seemed only imminent.

Neither of these arguments is conclusive, and so far we must be content with the limits given above. Only with regard to the Acts, I should be inclined to suggest that, judging by the early and undeveloped character of the religious phraseology, the complete absence of any developed form of organization, the absence of any allusion to the Pauline Epistles, and the favourable view held of the character of the civil government, we are not justified in placing it very late.

The date of St. Luke's Gospel, so far as it is settled, will help us to the date of St. Mark's. There are not many results of the modern study of the formation of the Gospel which are firmly established, but there are one or two on which we can rely. The old idea that St. Mark's Gospel was a shortened version of St. Matthew and St. Luke may be dismissed. We may accept it as certain that the common matter of the three Gospels was derived from an original which differed little if at all from St. Mark. I have no doubt myself that it was St. Mark. If this be so, it must date from a period earlier than the fall of Jerusalem. Irenaeus[1] tells us that after the death of St. Peter and St. Paul, Mark the disciple and interpreter of Peter, handed down to us in writing the things which had been announced by Peter. This, if true, would give the date shortly after the year 64, and the statement corresponds with all such internal evidence as we have. St. Luke's Gospel and St. Matthew's must both then be somewhat later.

Let us turn now to St. Matthew, and, to begin with, look at the external evidence that you have before you.[2] I have not referred to it with regard to St. Luke, St. Mark, or the Acts of the Apostles,

[1] Irenaeus, *In Omn. Nav.* III. 1, 2.

[2] See Appendix.

because, although what are probably quotations from or references to these books are to be found in the Apostolic Fathers, they are not sufficient to rely on. But when we turn to St. Matthew the case is, it seems to me, different. There are many quotations from the Gospel narrative, and almost all resemble the words of our present St. Matthew. It is quite true, of course, that the quotations are not always accurate, and that passages from different places have been grouped together, but the same writers quote the Old Testament inaccurately, and group together passages from the different Pauline Epistles. It is possible that the influence of oral tradition may be present in some cases, but substantially almost all the quotations resemble St. Matthew's Gospel more or less accurately. Either they come from St. Matthew or from another Gospel wonderfully like it, and it is quite contrary to the truest principles of criticism, when there is a quite adequate and satisfactory source in existence, to go out of our way to invent another document and discard that which we have before us.

One point more. There are in Ignatius two references to the Gospel narrative which have been held to be apocryphal. One is a passage in which our Lord is represented as saying after his resurrection: "Lay hold and handle me, and see that I am not a demon without body."[1] The other is as

[1] Ignatius, *Smyr.* 3.

follows: "A star shone forth in the heaven above all the stars; and its light was unutterable, and its strangeness caused amazement; and all the rest of the constellations with the sun and moon formed themselves into a chorus about the star; but the star itself far outshone them all; and there was perplexity to know whence came this strange appearance which was so unlike them. From that time forward every wrong and every spell was dissolved, the ignorance of wickedness vanished away, the ancient kingdom was pulled down, when God appeared in the likeness of man with *newness* of everlasting *life*; and that which had been perfected in the counsels of God began to take effect. Thence all things were perturbed because the abolishing of death was taken in hand."[1]

My own belief is that these passages arise from a somewhat vigorous imagination working on the narratives we possess. But suppose for a moment that they come from a Gospel which we do not possess. Then it must clearly be not a source or simpler form of the narrative, but a later working up. If Ignatius had another Gospel, those we possess must be very much earlier.

I believe then that our St. Matthew was used by Ignatius, Polycarp, the *Didache*, Barnabas, and probably Clement, and that its date therefore must be

[1] Ignatius, *Eph.* 19.

thrown well back into the first century. For more exact dating the evidence is precarious. The exact relation of the Eschatological passages to the events of 70 has been used to prove that the Gospel was written shortly before or after that year. The date is a probable one, but not certain, and I prefer for the present to be satisfied with the conclusion that it was written before the year 80, and with the general conclusion that the three Synoptic Gospels probably date from the years 60 to 80.

If we turn for just a moment to the internal evidence, there is one broad circumstance which I should like to bring before you as corroborating the early date both of the composition of the Gospels and their subject-matter, and that is their distinctly primitive character. There is an almost complete absence of any later theological terminology. Our Lord is ordinarily designated by the personal name Jesus. The term χριστὸς is never used as a personal name even as it is in St. Paul. You have only to compare these Gospels with the document called the Gospel of Peter to see the complete difference of character, and to be convinced of their comparatively early date.

There is just one more point to which I should like to refer. You will sometimes see it stated of the Gospels that they belong to this or that date with the exception of certain later additions. You will generally find that the passages suggested as later interpretations, are just those which happen to conflict with the writer's particular prejudices, but you naturally feel uneasy at the suggestion, and want to know whether there is any room for such suspicions. My own opinion is that there is not. The reason that I would give is as follows: We know pretty well the history of the text of the four Gospels back to the year 150, and we know that there were at that time at least two different types of text in existence. But the common parent of these texts takes us back to somewhere very near the archetype. And it is very unlikely that there should be many interpolations which are preserved in all the different documents supporting both these types of text. Textual criticism has probably already eliminated every verse and passage which were not part of the original text as they issued from the writer's hand. The attempts which have been made to mix up the lower and higher criticism have almost invariably failed.

To settle the dates of the Synoptic Gospels is only the first stage in a very difficult investigation; yet I believe, if we can agree to regard the limits of the dates I have named, 60—80, as correct, and will work backwards from then our study will be much more likely to be productive of results than if we entangle ourselves in the vagaries of a criticism that habitually puts everything impossibly late.

IV.

We pass now to the problems connected with the Johannine literature. There are five books associated with the name of John in the New Testament. The Apocalypse, the Fourth Gospel, and three Epistles. The intricacy of the problems they present turns on two questions. While a marked unity of style makes it clear that the Fourth Gospel and the three Epistles emanated from the same source, there are certainly very marked differences between these and the Apocalypse. But yet there is no need for thinking that these differences are fundamental, or impossible to reconcile with unity of authorship, for Professor Harnack, for example, although assigning none of these writings to the Apostle John, assigns them all to the same author, John the Presbyter. The second series of difficulties arise from the relations of the narrative in the Fourth Gospel to that in the other three.

Into these two questions I wish to enter as little as possible. Each of them could demand a lecture, or rather many lectures for themselves. I want rather to try and discover what external or internal evidences of date there may be which may perhaps give us a stable position from which to attack the more intricate problems.

Of the Apocalypse we have evidence both clear and

early. Justin Martyr, in his dialogue with Trypho, the Jew, written shortly after the year 150, mentions it as follows: "And afterwards also amongst us a certain man whose name was John, one of the apostles of the Christ, in a Revelation which came to him prophesied that those who believed in our Christ should pass a thousand years in Jerusalem, and after that there should be the universal and, to speak shortly, eternal resurrection of all men together and the judgment."[1] The words 'amongst us' naturally mean 'at Ephesus,' the scene of the dialogue, where Justin himself had lived some years before between the years 130 and 140. To this evidence of Justin we can add the more explicit testimony of Irenaeus. He tells us that "it is not long ago when it was written, but almost in our own generation, at the end of Domitian's reign." Elsewhere he quotes Rev. i. 12, 17, ascribing it to John the disciple of the Lord, and describes him as he who lay on the Lord's breast at supper.

The evidence, then, is that the Apocalypse was written in Asia by a person named John, who could be described as the apostle or disciple of the Lord, and that it was written at the close of Domitian's reign, that is during the years 90-96. It is interesting to note that this date is the conclusion to which criticism is strongly tending. While Baur and

[1] Justin, *Dialogue with Trypho*, 81.

those who followed him were inclined to assign the Apocalypse to the time of Nero, almost all modern writers have returned to the date which tradition had given. Of the exact identity of the author we shall speak later.

We now turn to the Gospel and Epistles.

1. The Gospel was known to Ignatius and read by him. This is, I believe, proved by the knowledge of the special teaching of St. John combined with a passage, the literary form of which implies a knowledge of the written Gospel. It has been said that these passages arise from a general acquaintance with the oral teaching which built up the Gospel. But let us remember, Ignatius, although he wrote in Asia, came from Antioch, and had not been brought up in the Christian school of Ephesus. His acquaintance with St. John's words must have been in writing, and the comparatively slight use made of them is quite consistent with the later date of this Gospel. Nor is the form of the quotation at all consistent with mere oral knowledge.

While Ignatius quotes the Gospel, Polycarp has a passage corresponding to the language of the Epistles, which he seems to quote or make use of in just the same way as he does the Pauline epistles.

You have these quotations before you. They may be explained away as every historical fact and statement from ancient times can be explained away.

But we have to ask ourselves not, How can I get over this evidence? but what is the most rational explanation of these facts?

2. A very definite ecclesiastical tradition ascribes the authorship of these documents to St. John, who, it is asserted, lived to the age of about 100, and died at Ephesus at the beginning of the reign of Trajan. "John, the disciple of the Lord, who lay upon his breast, himself gave forth the Gospel, when he was residing at Ephesus, in the province of Asia." So writes Irenaeus about the year 180. The value of the tradition is well known. Irenaeus was the pupil of Polycarp, and Polycarp the disciple of John. Irenaeus claims to give the information he had received directly on adequate authority. The evidence for this tradition may be summed up as follows: we have

(i.) The constant, clear testimony of Irenaeus.

(ii.) The corroborative evidence of Justin.

(iii.) The testimony of Polycartes, bishop of Ephesus in the year 196, who could point to the reputed tomb of John.

(iv.) The testimony of the Leucian Acts of John. These are apocryphal Acts of the Apostles, of which various fragments have been preserved. Their date is about 170. They are the work of a Gnostic heretic of Docetic, probably of Valentinian opinions. They are probably some of the most foolish books ever written. But that does not concern us. The important point is that they emanate from heretical sources, but that the writer clearly knows and makes use of St. John's Gospel, and that they assume the activity of St. John in Ephesus as axiomatic.

(v.) To these we can add the evidence of the Muratorian fragment on the Canon, of Clement of Alexandria and later fathers, perhaps coming from the sources we have enumerated, perhaps independent.

Now here we have a strong and decided body of evidence. What is to be said against it? An obscure passage in the writings of a certain Papias of Hierapolis, who lived about the year 140, has suggested to some persons that there were two people of the name of John in Asia at the close of the first century, namely John the Apostle and John the Presbyter, also called a disciple of the Lord. Some of the early Christian fathers who were by no means bad critics seized upon this suggestion, and a certain number of other hints, because it suggested a plausable theory for the authorship of the Apocalypse. They felt the difficulty of ascribing that work to the same author as the gospel, that is to the Apostle John, and assigned it to John the Presbyter; but none of them had any doubt about the gospel. This same John the Presbyter has been seized upon with alacrity by modern critics and widely exploited. Either he is considered to have been the author of the Fourth Gospel, while the Apocalypse is doubtfully ascribed to the Apostle, or the whole legend is maintained to have arisen from this confusion, and it is maintained that just as Philip the Apostle and Philip the Evangelist were confused together, so John the Presbyter and John the Apostle were confused. The Gospel then was written by John the Presbyter, and it is very doubtful indeed whether John the Apostle had anything to do with Asia and Ephesus.

We cannot, I am afraid, discuss this question fully. Let me point out this much, however, to begin with. This theory will not in any way simplify the problem of the Gospel. It is quite clear that that Gospel purports to have been written by John the Apostle either directly or indirectly. If it was not, it was forged by someone who wished it to be thought that it was. If John the Presbyter was (as Professor Harnack maintains) the author, you still have to assume that he had an acquaintance with the tradition delivered by John the Apostle, and really then it is not necessary to have a John the Presbyter at all. It is quite consistent with ecclesiastical tradition and the internal evidence of the Gospel that it should have been written down by the Christian circle which surrounded the Apostle. Nothing is gained as far as regards the Gospel by assuming another person of the name of John.

Moreover all the evidence concerning John the

Presbyter is very doubtful. The fact of his existence depends upon an obscure and possibly corrupt passage of Papias, as interpreted by Eusebius, who had an object in view. Many other early Christian writers had read Papias and none of them discovered the existence of the second John. All those who had read him believed that he testified to the existence of John the Apostle in Asia Minor. The writers who believed in John the Presbyter had no doubt that Papias testified also to John the Apostle, and although we cannot rely altogether on the accuracy of later quotations and references, we have definite statements quoted from Papias to the effect that the Fourth Gospel came from John the Apostle, but was written down at his dictation by Papias himself.[1]

What I would put before you is that a wide and early tradition ascribes the Gospel directly or indirectly to the Apostle John and gives us a clear idea of all the circumstances under which it was

[1] These are found in a preface to St. John's Gospel contained in the Codex Toletanus (Wordsworth and White, p. 490), see Burkitt, *Two Lectures on the Gospels*, pp. 68-70, 90-94. I quote the translation given by Mr. Burkitt: "this Gospel therefore it is manifest was written after the Apocalypse, and was given to the churches in Asia by John while he was yet in the body, as one Papias by name, Bishop of Hierapolis, a disciple of John and dear to him, in his *Exoterica, i.e.* in the end of the Five Books, related, he who wrote this Gospel at John's dictation (*Iohanne subdictante*)."

written, and that the internal evidence harmonizes with this. These facts have to be explained away, and the explanations given are neither convincing nor consistent.

3. I can only mention a third corroborative argument of early date. Exactly the same marks of early phraseology are characteristic of St. John's Gospel and the Synoptics. If you wish to realize the force of this you can compare the narrative in this Gospel with a recently discovered fragment of the Leucian Acts of John discovered by Dr. James of King's College, Cambridge. The letter is clearly an apocryphal document, and as far as it goes affords an admirable contrast to the simplicity, the early character, the religious sanity, and—if I may venture to say so—the inspired language of the First Gospel.

Let me sum up. There are quite clear indications of the use of the Johannine writings about the year 110. The traditions of the Ephesian evidences of the Apostle are strong and good. External and internal evidence both alike testify to the Apostle John being the author. I believe then that the Gospel and Epistles were written in Asia between the years 80 and 100, and come directly or indirectly from John the Apostle, the Apocalypse about 95 or 96, and if you like to believe that John the Presbyter wrote the latter, you may.

May I add one word in conclusion? There is an

impression in many quarters that the writers who are called apologists are continually building up elaborate and far-fetched theories to explain away what is obvious and natural, and that the simple and natural explanation of the facts is that of the newer critics. Throughout the Johannine question the reverse is the case. The simple and natural explanation is the orthodox one, it takes the facts simply as they are. It has far the most evidence in its favour. If you turn to the articles by Schmiedel and Abbott in the *Encyclopaedia Biblica*, you will find long and elaborate theories constructed to explain away simple facts. You will find what seem obvious quotations from St. John ascribed to Philo or some other writer to whose words they have only a distant resemblance. You will find every explanation but the natural one given of various passages. We will find a great deal that is clever and ingenious. But it is all of the nature of apologetics. The whole trend of investigation and discovery has been against the position adopted by those writers, and in much of what they say they are really in the position of an old-fashioned scholar defending the Pauline authorship of the Epistle to the Hebrews.

V.

The last group consists of four very difficult books. The Epistle of James has often been considered the oldest book in the New Testament. A reaction has now set in and it figures very often as one of the latest, being placed about the year 150. If it could be proved (as has been asserted) that it was quoted in the Epistle to the Romans the early date would be correct, but it cannot be so proved. There are no certain early quotations. There are similarities of expression to Clement's Epistle, but nothing that proves literary obligation. But I do not believe in the late date, and that for two reasons.

(1) The Epistle undoubtedly refers to a controversy about Faith and Works. We know that that controversy existed at a certain period in the first century; we have to invent it in the second. St. Paul's Epistles make it abundantly clear that there were within the Christian community many who did not accept his theory of Justification by Faith, and held that, like Abraham, Christians were justified by Works. This situation just suits the Epistle of James. But if we place it in the second century there is no natural place for it. "Perhaps," it is said, "in his polemic against faith the writer had in mind an ultra-Pauline gnosis, which he may or may not have disconnected from genuine Paulinism." But this is a situation of the existence of which we have no evidence, and which was certainly not natural at that time, for the Gnostic despised faith and exalted knowledge.

(2) Although Clement of Rome cannot be proved to have quoted the Epistle, it is quite clear that he was acquainted with and was indebted to the type of Christianity that it represents. Without really understanding the controversy, he attempted to harmonize, or at any rate unite, those who held justification by Faith and those who held justification by Works. We must suppose he had some other document of similar content if he had not the Epistle of James before him.

(3) The ecclesiastical situation and language do not exhibit anything which must be late, and have some features which must be early.

The natural date for it is the time of the Pauline controversy, the natural place Jerusalem, the natural author the writer by whom it claims to have been written. By whom and at what time it was translated, to what agency it owes its gnomic and impressive language, what has been its history we do not know. A forger generally has a purpose, but the Epistle of James became an anachronism long before any date when it could have been forged.

The First Epistle of Peter is one of the best attested books of the New Testament. Although the Apostolic Fathers never quote it under any name, it was as well known to them as were the Pauline Epistles. It contains no evidence of later date. Its theological language is simple and early.

On the one hand, it must have been written after the Romans and Ephesians, to which it is indebted ; on the other hand, it must have been earlier than the time of Clement. It was written from Rome, it claims to have been by Peter, and there is nothing in the contents to compel us to put it later than the year 464 A.D., although we cannot perhaps prove that it was earlier than 80-90.

The Second Epistle of Peter and the Epistle of Jude are the most doubtful writings in the New Testament. There is no external testimony to compel us to put them before 150 A.D., but that does not of course necessarily compel us to put them so late. It may well be that such short and unimportant books might miss being quoted in the few writings we possess. Their relationship to one another is undetermined. There are many passages in both which make their genuineness seem doubtful. There is such a marked difference of style between the two Epistles of St. Peter that we can only suppose both to be genuine by assuming a different translator. On the other hand, there is nothing in them which need be later than the first century. I cannot claim to have studied them sufficiently to give a more definite opinion of my own.

The object which we set before ourselves at the beginning of this lecture was not to attempt a detailed dating of the separate books, but to keep steadily in view the main question, whether the traditional view according to which the books of the New Testament were written in the first century was correct. Our aim will have been satisfied, if I have succeeded in making it clear that those who hold this traditional view have a very strong case indeed, a case which on all points, except one or two, has steadily grown stronger with the advance of knowledge. It is significant that Professor Harnack, whose views of Christianity are certainly not orthodox, has recognized this ; it is significant again that Professor Gardner considers that there is no reason why all the books of the New Testament should not have been written before the close of the first century. These opinions are not indeed universal, but the late dates still accepted by some critics are, I believe, an anachronism. The careful investigation and accurate dating of the documents of the second century, and especially of the Apostolic Fathers, have made writings, like those of Professor Schmiedel and Dr. Abbott, as much behind the times as the Greek Testament of Bishop Christopher Wordsworth.

Do not imagine for a moment that I should claim that the controversy was over. The credibility and historical character of the New Testament writings still demands much investigation. But for the future the living defence of traditional Christianity and the living attack—the defence such as that of Dr. Sanday and Dr. Strong, the attack such as that of Professor Harnack and Professor Gardiner—will accept substantially the same dates. At the threshold of the future questions: How far are the New Testament books credible? What ultimate answer can we give when asked, What think ye of Christ; whose son is He? my task ends; only to any who would ask for some provisional answer I would say; The dates of the Epistle to the Romans and the first Epistle to the Corinthians are within a year or two absolutely certain. Their genuineness may be considered undisputed. Read them, and grasp their meaning and all that they imply. Then compare them with the Old Testament, and with the contemporary Jewish literature, and with classical literature, if you do so you will realize what a tremendous interval separates them from anything which had appeared in the world before. Try and conceive what cause could have been sufficient within a very few years to create such a wonderful new world of thought and ideas and institutions, of moral motive and religious aspirations. Then you will begin to understand the problem of early Christianity, and perhaps, if one comprehends the problem, the solution necessarily follows.

APPENDIX.[1]

QUOTATIONS FROM THE NEW TESTAMENT IN THE WRITINGS OF THE APOSTOLIC FATHERS.

THE following quotations are all taken from writings which represent the first quarter of the second century or an earlier period. These are:

(1) *The Epistle of* CLEMENT *to the Corinthian Church* (Clem.). (About 95 A.D.)

(2) *The* DIDACHE (Did.) or *Teaching of the Twelve Apostles*, a composite document. (80–110 A.D.)

(3) *The Epistle of* BARNABAS (Barn.). (70–120 A.D.)

(4) *The Epistle of* IGNATIUS (Ign.). (About 110 A.D.)

(5) *The Epistle of* POLYCARP (Pol.). (About 110 A.D.)

The extracts are grouped as follows:

I. General Statements.
II. The Pauline Epistles.
III. The Epistle to the Hebrews.
IV. The Acts and the Synoptic Gospels.
V. The Johannine Writings.
VI. The Remaining Books.

[1] The courtesy of the Lightfoot Trustees in permitting the use of Bishop Lightfoot's Translation of the Apostolic Fathers is gratefully acknowledged.

H. H. H.

I. General Statements.

To the writers of this period, as to the writers of the New Testament, the Scriptures are naturally the Old Testament. The words of our Lord are quoted with such formulas as 'remembering the words of the Lord Jesus' (Clem. 13, 46), 'remembering the words which the Lord spake, as he taught' (Pol. 2); 'according as the Lord said' (Pol. 7). Occasionally there are references directly to an Epistle of St. Paul, but generally the quotations from the Epistles, which are by far the most numerous, are made without acknowledgment. In certain passages, however, there are approximations to later uses.

(1) Pol. 12. 'For I am persuaded that ye are well trained *in the sacred writings*, and nothing is hidden from you. But to myself this is not granted. Only, as it is said in these Scriptures, *Be ye angry and sin not*, and *Let not the sun set on your wrath.*'

The first quotation comes from *Ps.* iv. 4, and is quoted in *Eph.* iv. 26; the second comes from *Eph.* iv. 26. The Old Testament quotation may have made it easier to speak of St. Paul's writings as scripture, but this early instance of later phraseology is quite consistent with Polycarp's whole attitude to the New Testament. He uses the writings as if they were his Bible.

(2) Ign. *Phil.* 5, 'taking refuge in the *Gospel* as the flesh of Jesus, and in the *Apostles* as the presbytery of the Church. Yea, and we love the Prophets also, because they too pointed to the Gospel.'

There is clearly a reference to writings, and to authoritative writings of Apostles as corresponding to the Prophets; but it is very doubtful if the word Gospel can be proved here to mean a 'book,' it probably still means 'the message.' So *Smyrn.* 7. 'It is therefore meet that ye should abstain from such, and not speak of them either privately or in public ; but should give heed to the Prophets, and especially to the *Gospel*, wherein the passion is shown unto us and the resurrection is accomplished.' Cf. also *Phil.* 9.

(3) Barn. 4. Let us give heed, lest haply we be found, *as the Scripture saith*, *Many called but few chosen*.

Here we have *Matth.* xxii. 14 quoted with the ordinary formula for the citation of Scripture. It is possible to press it too far, but that the point is significant is shown by the bold effort made to explain it away. See, for example, Dr. Abbott in *Encyclopaedia Biblica* II., 1828, who thinks that perhaps it is a quotation from Enoch ; but as the passage does not occur in Enoch as we know it, he has to suppose another recension. This represents a most elaborate and far-fetched method of apology.

(4) Did. 8. Neither pray ye *as the hypocrites*, but as the Lord commanded in His *Gospel*, *thus pray ye* : *Our Father*, etc.

Ib. 15. And reprove one another, not in anger but in peace, as ye find in the *Gospel*. . . . But your prayers and your almsgiving and all your deeds, so do ye as you find it in the *Gospel* of our Lord.

In both these passages the word Gospel has come very near to meaning a written Gospel.

II. The Pauline Epistles.

(1) *Romans*. There is no reference to this Epistle by name, yet the following passage in Ignatius' letter to the Roman Church may have been suggested by it: 'I do not enjoin you as Peter and Paul did. They were Apostles, I am a convict ; they were free, but I am a slave to this very hour' (Ign. *Rom.* 4). But the quotations in Clement of Rome are numerous, as also in Polycarp. The resemblances of language in Ignatius, which, as is so often the case, do not rise to the dignity of a quotation, are perhaps even more

significant. There are also quotations or reminiscences in the Didache and in Barnabas. The following two instances will suffice for our purpose.

1 Clem. 35, Casting off from ourselves all *unrighteousness* and iniquity, *covetousness*, *strifes*, *malignities* and *deceits*, *whisperings* and *backbitings*, *hatred of God*, *pride* and *arrogance*, vainglory and inhospitality. For they *that do these things* are hateful to God; and *not only they that do them*, but *they also that consent* unto them.	*Rom.* I 29-32. Being filled with all *unrighteousness*, fornication, wickedness, *covetousness*, maliciousness; full of envy, murder, debate, *deceit*, *malignity*; *whisperers*, *backbiters*, *haters of God*, despiteful, *proud*, *boasters*, inventors of evil things, disobedient to parents, without understanding, covenant-breakers, without natural affection, implacable; unmerciful; who knowing the judgment of God, that they which commit such things are worthy of death, *not only do the same*, *but have pleasure in them that do them*.
Pol. 6. For we are before the eyes of our Lord and God, and we must *all stand at the Judgment-Seat of Christ*, and *each man must give an account* of *himself*.	*Rom.* xiv. 10. For *we* shall *all stand before the Judgment-Seat* of God.. (cf. 2 Cor. v. 10.) 12. So then *each one of us shall give account* of *himself* to God.

We notice that the second passage is quoted without the words τῷ θεῳ which are omitted by B and some other authorities.

For further instances see Sanday and Headlam, *Romans*, p. lxxx.

(2) I *Corinthians*. This Epistle is definitely referred to by name in the Letter of Clement to the Corinthians, written 40 years later.

1. Clem. 47. 'Take up *the epistle of the blessed Paul the Apostle*. What wrote he first unto you in the beginning of the Gospel?

Of a truth he charged you in the spirit concerning himself and Cephas and Apollos, because that even then ye had made parties.'

Reminiscences of the Epistle are numerous. Such are found in Clement, Ignatius, Polycarp, and in the Didache. The following instances will probably suffice.

Ign. *Eph.* 1. My spirit is made an offscouring for the Cross, which is a *stumbling-block* to them that are unbelievers, *but to us* salvation and life eternal. *Where is the wise? Where is the disputer?* Where is the *boasting* of them that are called *prudent?*	1 *Cor.* i. 18-20. For the preaching of the cross is to them that perish foolishness; but *unto* us which are saved it is the power of God. 19. For it is written, I will destroy the wisdom of the *wise*, and will bring to nothing the understanding of the *prudent*. 20. *Where is the wise?* Where is the scribe? *Where is the disputer* of this world? Hath not God made foolish the wisdom of this world?
1 Clem. 34. For he saith, *Eye hath not seen* and *ear hath not heard*, and it *hath not entered into the heart of man* what great *things He hath prepared* for them that patiently await Him.	1 *Cor.* ii. 9. But as it is written, *Eye hath not seen*, *nor ear heard*, *neither have entered into the heart of man*, the *things* which God hath *prepared for them* that love him.

St Paul quotes freely *Is.* xliv. 4. 'Clement mixes up St Paul's free translation or paraphrase from the Hebrew with the passage as it stands in the LXX.' Ltf.

Pol. 11. If a man refrain not from covetousness, he shall be defiled by idolatry, and shall be judged as one of the Gentiles who know not the judgment of the Lord. *Nay, know we not, that the saints shall judge the world, as Paul teacheth?*	1 *Cor.* vi. 2. *Do ye not know that the saints shall judge the world?*

Here again we have 1 *Cor.* definitely cited as being by St. Paul.

Pol. 5. And *neither whoremongers nor effeminate persons, nor defilers of themselves with men, shall inherit the kingdom of God*, neither they that do untoward things.	1 *Cor.* vi. 9, 10. Be not deceived: *neither fornicators*, nor idolaters, nor adulterers, *nor effeminate, nor abusers of themselves with men*, nor thieves, nor covetous, nor drunkards, nor revilers, nor extortioners, *shall inherit the kingdom of God.*

In Pol. 5 there is a reminiscence of 1 *Cor.* xiv. 25, and in Pol. 10 from 1 *Cor.* xv. 58.

(3) 2 *Corinthians.* Quotations from the Second Epistle to the Corinthians are much less numerous.

Pol. 11. But I have not found any such thing in you, neither have heard thereof, among whom the *blessed Paul laboured*, who were his *epistles* in the beginning.	2 *Cor.* iii. 2. Ye are our *epistle*, written in our hearts, known and read of all men.

Although the quotation is slight, it is too significant to be doubtful.

Pol. 2. Now *He that raised Him* from the dead *will raise us also.*	2 *Cor.* iv. 14. Knowing that *he which raised up* the Lord Jesus *shall raise up us also* with Jesus.

In Pol. 6 there is a reminiscence of 2 *Cor.* viii. 26.

(4) *Galatians.*

Pol. 5. Knowing then that *God is not mocked*, we ought to walk worthily of His commandment and His glory.	*Gal.* vi. 7. Be not deceived; *God is not mocked*: for whatsoever a man soweth, that shall he also reap.

In Pol. 12, *Gal.* i. 1 is quoted; in Pol. 3, *Gal.* iv. 26.

(5) *Ephesians.*

Ign. *Eph.* 12. Ye are associates in the mysteries with Paul, who was sanctified, who obtained a good report, who is worthy of all felicitation ; in whose footsteps I would fain be found treading, when I shall attain unto God ; *who in every letter* maketh mention of you in Christ Jesus.

This ought perhaps rather to be quoted as a reference to a general collection of Pauline letters. St. Paul refers to the Ephesians in six of his Epistles. Quotations from this Epistle are numerous.

Pol. 1. Forasmuch as ye know that it is *by grace ye are saved*, *not by works*, but by the will of God through Christ Jesus.

Eph. ii. 8, 9. For *by grace are ye saved* through faith ; and that not of yourselves : it is the gift of God : *not of works*, lest any man should boast.

1 Clem. 46. Have we not *one God* and *one Christ* and *one Spirit of grace* that was shed upon us? And is there not *one calling in Christ?*

Eph. iv. 4. There is one body, and *one Spirit*, even as ye are called in *one hope of your calling;* one Lord, one faith, one baptism, *one God* and Father of all, who is above all, and through all, and in you all. But unto every one of us is *given grace* according to the measure of the gift of Christ.

Pol. 10. *Be ye all subject one to another.*

Eph. v. 21. *Subjecting yourselves one to another* in the fear of Christ.

There is also a reminiscence of *Eph.* vi. 18 in Pol. 12. For the quotation of *Eph.* iv. 26, see above, p. 184

Ign. *Pol.* 5. In like manner also charge my brothers in the

Eph. v. 25. Husbands, love your wives, *even as Christ also*

name of Jesus Christ to love their wives, *as the Lord the Church.*

loved the church and gave himself for it. . . .

29. . . . but nourisheth and cherisheth it, *even as the Lord the church.*

(6) *Philippians.* A letter or letters of St. Paul to the Philippians is referred to in the following passage from Polycarp. Pol. 3: 'For neither am I, nor is any other like unto me, able to follow the wisdom of the blessed and glorious Paul, who when he came among you taught face to face with the men of that day the word which concerneth truth carefully and surely; who also when he was absent wrote letters unto you, into the which if you look diligently, ye shall be able to be builded up unto the faith given to you.'

The plural may
either (1) be the Epistolary plural, meaning only one letter.
or (2) include letters to the Thessalonians.
or (3) include other letters to the Philippians not now preserved.

Quotations from the epistle are neither numerous nor important.

Pol. 9. Being persuaded that all these *ran not in vain* but in faith and righteousness.

Phil. ii. 16. That I did *not run in vain,* neither labour in vain.

The words are exactly the same in both passages. There is a reminiscence of *Phil.* iii. 18 in Pol. 12.

(7) *Colossians.*

Quotations or reminiscences of the *Colossians* are also very uncommon; the following is definite as far as it goes.

Ign. *Eph.* 10. Against their errors be ye *stedfast in the faith.*

Col. i. 23. If so be that ye continue *in the faith grounded and stedfast.*

(8) 1 *and* 2 *Thessalonians.*

Here again the quotations are slight.

Ign. *Eph.* 10. And *pray* also *without ceasing* for the rest of mankind.	1 *Thess.* v. 17. *Pray without ceasing.*
Pol. 11. For he *boasteth of* you in all those *churches* which alone at that time knew *God.*	2 *Thess.* i. 4. So that we ourselves *boast of you* in the *churches of God.*

The allusion is to *Phil.* i. 3, 4, iv. 10, 18, but the language is taken from 2 *Thess.* Immediately before he has written of the Philippians as "the letters" of St. Paul from the beginning, taking his language from 2 *Cor.* iii. 2 (see page 188).

Pol. 11. Be ye therefore yourselves also sober herein, and *hold not such as enemies*, but restore them as frail and erring members.	2 *Thess.* iii. 15. And yet *count him not as an enemy*, but admonish him as a brother.

(9) *The Pastoral Epistles.*

1 Clem. 7. And let us see what is *good*, and what is pleasant and what is *acceptable in the sight of* Him that made us.	1 *Tim.* ii. 3. For this is *good* and *acceptable in the sight of* God our Saviour.
Pol. 4. But *the love of money* is the beginning of *all* troubles. Knowing therefore that *we brought nothing into the world neither can we carry anything out.*	1 *Tim.* vi. 10. For *the love of money* is the root of *all* evil. 1 *Tim.* vi. 7. *For we brought nothing into the world*, for *neither can we carry anything out.*

In Pol. 12 there is a reference to 1 *Tim.* ii. 1 and to 1 *Tim.* iv. 15.

Pol. 5. If we conduct ourselves worthily of Him, *we shall also reign with Him*, if indeed we have faith.	2 *Tim.* ii. 12. If we endure *we shall also reign with him* : if we shall deny him, he also will deny us.

Pol. 9. For they *loved not the present world*, but Him that died for our sakes and was raised by God for us.

2 *Tim.* iv. 10. For Demas forsook me, having *loved* this *present world.*

1 Clem. 2. Ye repented not of any well-doing, but were *ready unto every good work.*

Tit. iii. 1. Put them in mind . . . to be ready *to every good work.*

The above instances show that reminiscences of or coincidences with the Pastoral Epistles are numerous, in Ignatius particularly there are constant parallels in thought as in expression, but they are not of a sufficiently definite character to be called quotations.

There are no resemblances to *Philemon* worth mentioning.

III. The Epistle to the Hebrews.

The Epistle to the Hebrews must have been well known to the writer of the Epistle of Clement. There are over twenty places in which there are resemblances of language, and several where the resemblances become quotations. The work is never mentioned by name. Elsewhere there is a clear resemblance of language in the Didache, and both Ignatius and Polycarp use the title High Priest of our Lord, a title only found in the Hebrews. The following instances from Clement will, however, be seen to be conclusive.

1 Clem. 36. 2, 3, 4, 5. *Who being the effulgence* of His Majesty is so *much greater than angels, as He hath inherited a more excellent name.* For so it is written: *who maketh His angels spirits and His Ministers a flame of fire: but of His Son* the Master

Heb. i. 3-5. *Who being the effulgence* of his glory, and the very image of his substance, and upholding all things by the word of his power, when he had made purification of sins, sat down on the right hand of the Majesty on high, *having become*

said thus: *Thou art My Son this day have I begotten Thee.* Ask of Me, and I will give Thee the Gentiles for Thine inheritance, and the ends of the earth for Thy possession. And again He saith unto Him: *Sit Thou on My right hand, until I make Thine enemies a footstool for Thy feet.*

so much better than the angels, as he hath inherited a more excellent name than they. For unto which of the angels said he at any time, *Thou art my Son. This day have I begotten thee.* . . .

7. And of the angels he saith, *Who maketh his angels winds, and his ministers a flame of fire: but of the Son* he saith, Thy throne O God is for ever and ever, etc. . . .

13. But of which of the angels hath he said at any time: *Sit thou on my right hand till I make thine enemies the footstool of thy feet.*

1 Clem. 17. Let us be imitators of them which went *about in goatskins and sheepskins*, preaching the coming of Christ. We mean Elijah and Elisha and likewise Ezekiel, the prophets, and besides them those *men that obtained a good report.* Abraham obtained an exceeding *good report* and was called the friend of God; and looking steadfastly on the glory of God, he saith in lowliness of mind, But I am dust and ashes.

Heb. xi. 37. They wandered *about in sheepskins, in goatskins.*

39. And these all *having obtained a good report* through faith.

Cf. 2, 4, 5.

The thought also of v. 10, 16 has suggested the idea of Abraham looking steadfastly to the glory of God.

1 Clem. 9. Let us set before us Enoch, who being found righteous in obedience *was translated*, and his death was not found. Noah, being found *faith-*

Heb. xi. 5. By faith Enoch was translated that he should not see death; and was not found because God had translated him; for before his trans-

ful, by his ministration preached regeneration unto the world, and through him the Master saved the living creatures that entered into the ark in concord.

lation he had this testimony, that he pleased God. . . .

7. By faith, Noah being warned of God of things not seen as yet, moved with fear, prepared an ark to the saving of his house; by the which he condemned the world, and became heir of the righteousness, which is by faith.

See also the instances of Abraham, 1 Clem. 10, of Rahab, 1 Clem. 12.

Did. 4. My child, thou shalt *remember* him *that speaketh unto thee, the word of God* night and day, and shalt honour him as the Lord.

Heb. xiii. 7. *Remember* them which have the rule over you, *which spake unto you the word of God.*

IV. The Acts and Synoptic Gospels.

(1) *The Acts.* Quotations from the Acts are slight, but not altogether unimportant.

Ign. *Mgn.* 5. Each man shall *go to his own place.*

Acts i. 25. From which Judas fell away that he might *go to his own place.*

The phrase is exactly the same in both, but it might of course be a proverbial expression, used independently by both writers.

Pol. 1. Our Lord Jesus Christ, who endured to face even death for our sins, *whom God raised, having loosed the pangs of Hades.*

Acts ii. 24. *Whom God raised up, having loosed the pangs of death.*

27. Because thou wilt not leave my soul in *Hades.*

The quotation is almost exact, the word ἤγειρεν (raised) being substituted for ἀνέστησεν (raised up), and Hades for death, a reminiscence of v. 27.

Did. 4. Thou shalt not turn away from him that is in want, but shalt make thy brother partaker in all things, and shalt not say *that anything is thine own.*

Barn. 19, 8. Thou shalt make thy neighbour partaker in all things, and shalt not say *that anything is thine own.*

Acts iv. 32. And not one of them said that ought of the things which he possessed *was his own.*

This quotation (if such it be) presumably comes from the common document that underlies the Didache and Barnabas.

Ign. *Smyrn.* 3. *And after His resurrection* He *ate with them* and *drank with* them as one in the flesh, though spiritually He was united with the Father.

Acts x. 41. To us who *did eat and drink* with him *after he rose from* the dead.

The Greek words are the same in both passages, only the person is changed.

Pol. 2. Who cometh as *judge of quick and dead.*

Acts x. 42. This is he which was ordained of God to be the *judge of quick and dead.*

It is obvious that not much stress can be laid on this; the phrase *judge of quick and dead* must have been a common Christian formula very early. (cf. 2 Tim. iv. 1.)

1 Clem. 2. *More glad to give than to receive.*

1 Clem. 13. Most of all *remembering the words of the Lord Jesus* which He spake.

Acts xx. 35. And to *remember the words of the Lord Jesus,* how he said, It is more blessed *to give than to receive.*

Here again we may have an independent knowledge of the words of our Lord, yet the separate quotations of the two different parts of the passage in the *Acts* suggests a literary obligation.

(2) *The Synoptic Gospels.* It will be convenient first of all to group together a number of passages which have been held to show a knowledge of the contents of the Gospel and not any special Gospel.

Pol. 12. *Pray for all the saints. Pray* also *for kings* and powers and princes, and for *them that persecute* and *hate you,* and *for the enemies of the cross,* that your fruit *might be manifest among all men,* that ye may be *perfect* in Him.

Matt. v. 44. *Pray for them that persecute you,* that ye may be the sons of your Father which is in heaven . . .

48. Ye therefore shall be *perfect,* as your heavenly Father is *perfect.*

Cf. *Luke* vi. 27. Do good to them which *hate you,* bless them that curse you, pray for them that despitefully use you.

This is a very composite passage ; phrases are taken from *Eph.* vi. 18 (supplication *for all the Saints*), 1 *Tim.* ii. 1 (*prayers . . . for kings* and all that are in high places), *Phil.* iii. 18 (*enemies of the cross* of Christ), 1 *Tim.* iv. 15 (that thy prayers *may be manifest unto all*). The word *perfect* makes the reference to Matt. v. 44, 48 or some very similar document almost certain, and there is no need to assume any reference to St. Luke. This passage has been put first because it shows very clearly the way in which the language of Polycarp is built up out of New Testament phrases without either exact or full quotations. We may assume that he used the Gospels as he certainly used the Epistles, and verbal differences or the combination of separate passages will not necessarily imply the use of a different Gospel.

Pol. 2. And again *blessed are the poor and they that are persecuted for righteousness' sake ; for theirs is the kingdom of God.*

Matt. v. 3. *Blessed are the poor* in spirit *for theirs is the kingdom of heaven.*

Luke. vi. 20. *Blessed are ye poor : for yours is the kingdom of God.*

Matt. v. 10. *Blessed are they that have been persecuted for righteousness' sake: for theirs is the kingdom of heaven.*

This might come from St. Matthew or St. Luke, or from some similar source. The phrase 'kingdom *of God*' might imply a knowledge of some other document besides St. Matthew.

Pol. 7. Entreating the all-seeing God with supplications that He *bring us not into temptation*, according as the Lord said, *The spirit indeed is willing, but the flesh is weak.*

Matt. vi. 13. And *bring us not into temptation.*

Cf. *Luke* xi. 4.

Matt. xxvi. 41. *The spirit indeed is willing, but the flesh is weak.*

Cf. *Mark* xiv. 38.

In the first citation, the resemblance both in St. Mark and St. Luke is exact, but it is obvious that no stress can be laid on the quotation, as it may be presumed that the Lord's Prayer was already in use among Christians. In the second quotation, St. Matthew and St. Mark agree exactly, so that it is impossible to say from which the quotation comes. It is also again conceivable that it came from a common source, if there was one. But St. Matthew's Gospel is a quite sufficient source for both passages.

1 Clem. 13. Most of all remembering the words of the Lord Jesus which He spake, teaching forbearance and long suffering: for thus He spake:

Have *mercy* that ye may receive *mercy*; forgive, that it may be forgiven to you. As ye do, so shall it be done to you. As ye give, so shall it be given unto you. *As ye judge, so shall ye be judged.* As ye show kindness, so shall kindness be showed unto you. *With what measure ye mete, it shall be measured withal to you.*

Pol. 2. But remembering the words which the Lord spake, and He taught: *Judge not, that ye be not judged.* Forgive and it will be forgiven to you. Have *mercy* that ye may receive *mercy. With what measure ye mete, it shall be measured to you again.*

Matt. vii. 1, 2. *Judge not, that ye be not judged.* For with what judgement ye judge, ye shall be judged: *and with what measure ye mete, it shall be measured unto you.*

Luke vi. 36-38. Be ye *merciful, even* as your Father is *merciful. And judge* not, and ye shall not be *judged*: and condemn not, and ye shall not be condemned: release, and ye shall be released: give, and it shall be given unto you: good measure, pressed down, shaken together, running over, shall they give into your bosom. *For with what measure ye mete, it shall be measured to you again.*

See also *Math.* vi. 14, 15.

The variations from the language of our Gospels and the resemblance between the quotation in Clement and that in Polycarp may be taken to show:

(1) That the quotations were then unwritten tradition.
or (2) That the writers had another and earlier form of the Gospel narrative.

But (1) this is one of the passages in which Polycarp shows a knowledge of Clement.

(2) The deviations from the Gospel narrative are not in the direction of a simpler form, but of greater elaboration. They could be quite adequately explained as a free working up of documents which we possess, in the same manner as in other quotations and adaptations in Polycarp and Clement.

1 Clem. 46. Remember the words of Jesus our Lord: for He said, *Woe unto that man; it were good for him if he had not been*

born, rather *than* that he should *offend one of* Mine elect. It *were better for* him *that a mill stone were hanged* about him, *and he cast into the sea*, *than* that he should pervert one of Mine elect.

This comes from two places :

(1) *Matt.* xxvi. 14 = *Mark* xiv. 21. *Woe unto that man* by whom the Son of man is betrayed! *it had been good for that man if he had not been born*.

Luke xxii. 22. But woe unto that man by whom he is betrayed.

Here the resemblance is closest with the first passage.

(2) *Matt.* xviii. 6, 7. But whoso *shall offend* one of these little ones which believe in me, it were better for him that *a mill stone were hanged about* his neck, and that he were *drowned in the depths of the sea*. Woe unto the world because of offences! for it must needs be that offences come : but *woe to that man* by whom the offence cometh.

Mark ix. 42. And whosoever *shall offend one* of these little ones that believe in me, *it is better for him that a mill stone were hanged about* his neck, and he were cast into the sea.

Luke xvii. 1, 2. It is impossible but that offences will come : but *woe unto him* by whom they come! It were better for him that a mill stone were hanged about his neck, and he cast into the sea, than that he should offend one of these little ones.

Here the resemblance is most clearly to St. Matthew, and there is one remarkable word καταποντισθῆναι which one might naturally suppose was drawn thence. There is a slight resemblance in the form of the sentence which might suggest that St. Luke had been used, but no stress can be laid upon it.

The only marked contrast with the Gospel narrative is the use of the word 'elect' for 'little ones.' (cf. Mk. xiii. 22.)

1 Clem. 24. *The sower goeth forth* and casteth into the earth each of the seeds ; and these falling into the earth dry and bear decay : then out of their decay the mightiness of the Master's providence raiseth them up, and from being one they increase manifold and bear fruit.

The first words are clearly a reminiscence of the Gospel narrative, but the words ἐξῆλθεν ὁ σπείρων occur in exactly the same form in all the Gospels.

Did. 1. The way of life is this. First of all, *thou shalt love the God* that made thee; secondly, *thy neighbour as thyself. And all things whatsoever thou wouldest not have befal thyself, neither do thou unto another.* Now of these words the doctrine is this. *Bless them that curse you,* and *pray* for your enemies, and fast for them that *persecute you: for what thank is it, if ye love them that love you? Do not even the Gentiles the same? But do ye love them that hate you,* and ye shall not have an enemy. Abstain thou from fleshy and bodily lusts. *If any man give thee a blow on thy right cheek, turn to him the other also,* and thou shalt be *perfect;* if a man *compel thee to go with him one mile, go with him twain; if a man take away thy cloak, give him thy coat also;* if a man take away from thee that which is thine own, ask it not back, for neither art thou able; *to every man that asketh of thee give,* and ask not back.

Matt. xxii. 37, 39. *Thou shalt love the Lord thy God* with all thy heart.

39. Thou shalt love *thy neighbour as thyself.*

Matt. v. 44. Love your enemies, pray for them *that persecute you.*

46. *For if ye love them that love you,* what *reward have you, do not even* the publicans *the same.*

Luke vi. 27. Love your enemies; do good to them that hate you.

32. *And if ye love them that love you,* what *thank have ye, for even* sinners *love those* that love them.

35. But *love* your enemies.

Matt. v. 39. Whosoever smiteth thee *on thy right cheek, turn to him the other also.*

40. *And if any man would go to law mith thee, and take away thy coat, let him have thy cloak also.*

41. *And whosoever shall compel thee to go one mile, go with him twain.*

42. *Give to him that asketh of thee,* and from him that would borrow of thee turn not thou away.

Luke vi. 30. *Give to every one that asketh thee: and of him that taketh away thy goods, ask them not again.*

(3) *St. Matthew's Gospel.*

Did. 1. Woe to him that receiveth; for if a man receiveth having need, he is guiltless; but he that hath no need shall give satisfaction why and wherefore he received; and being put in confinement, he shall be examined concerning the deeds that he hath done, *and he shall not come out thence until he hath paid the last farthing.* Yea, as touching this also it is said: Let thine alms sweat into thine hands until thou shalt have learnt to whom to give.

Matt. v. 25. Verily, I say unto thee, *thou shalt by no means come out thence, till thou have paid the last farthing.*

It can hardly be doubted that the passage in St. Matthew is in its original context and not that in the Didache.

Did. 9. But let no one eat or drink of this eucharistic thanksgiving, but they that have been baptized into the name of the Lord; for concerning this also the Lord hath said: *Give not that which is holy unto the dogs.*

Matt. vii. 6. *Give not that which is holy unto the dogs.*

Here St. Matthew's Gospel and not the Didache gives the original setting.

Ign. *Smyrn.* 1. Baptized by John that *all righteousness might be fulfilled* by Him.

Matt. iii. 15. Suffer it now, for thus it becometh us to *fulfil all righteousness.*

This quite clearly comes from St. Matthew.

Ign. *Smyrn.* 6. He that *receiveth, let him receive.*

Matt. xix. 12. He that is able to *receive* it, *let him receive it.*

Ign. *Pol.* 2. *Be thou* prudent as the *serpent* in all things and guileless always *as the dove.*

Matt. x. 16. Be ye therefore wise as *serpents* and harmless as *doves.*

Ign. *Eph.* 14. *The tree is manifest from its fruit*; so they that profess to be Christ's shall be seen through their actions.

Matt. xii. 33. *For the tree is known by its fruit.*

Did. 7. But concerning baptism, thus shall ye baptize. Having first recited all these things, baptize *in the name of the Father, and of the Son, and of the Holy Spirit* in living water.

See *Matt.* xxviii. 17. But the formula might of course be known independently of the Gospel, and probably existed earlier.

Did. 8. Neither pray ye *as the hypocrites*, but as the Lord commanded in His Gospel, thus pray ye: *Our Father which art in heaven, hallowed be Thy name; Thy kingdom come; Thy will be done, as in heaven, so also on earth; give us this day our daily bread; and forgive us our debt, as we also forgive our debtors; and lead us not into temptation, but deliver us from the evil one, for Thine is the power and the glory, for ever and ever.* Three times in the day pray ye so.

See *Matt.* vi. 16, vi. 9-13. The slight allusion to the hypocrites seems conclusive as to the source.

(4) *St. Mark.*

Pol. 5. Walking according to the truth of the Lord, who became a *minister of all.*

Mark ix. 35. And he saith unto them, If any man would be first, he shall be last of all, and *minister of all.*

The particular phrase πάντων διάκονος occurs only in St. Mark. In Pol. it is διάκονος πάντων. This is perhaps the only quotation in the Apostolic Fathers which seems to imply the knowledge of St. Mark's Gospel, and this may perhaps be accidental.

(5) *St. Luke.*

Did. 16. *Be watchful* for your life: *let your lamps not be quenched, and your loins not un-*

Matt. xxv. 13. *Watch therefore*, for ye know not the day nor the hour.

girded, but be ye ready; for ye know not the hour in which our Lord cometh.

Luke xii. 35. *Let your loins be girded about, and your lamps burning.*

40. *Be ye also ready*, for in *an hour* that ye think not the Son of Man cometh.

Matt. xxiv. 42. Watch therefore: *for ye know not* on what day your Lord cometh.

The passage seems to imply a reminiscence of St. Luke's Gospel, as well as St. Matthew's.

V. The Johannine Writings.

(1) *The Gospel.*

Ign. *Phil.* 7. For even though certain persons desired to deceive me after the flesh, yet *the spirit* is not deceived, being from God: for *it knoweth whence it cometh and where it goeth*, and it searcheth out the hidden things.

John iii. 8. The wind bloweth where it listeth, and thou hearest the voice thereof, *but knowest not whence it cometh, and whither it goeth*: so is every one that is born of the *spirit.*

John viii. 14. Jesus answered and said unto them, Even if I bear witness of myself, my witness is true: for I know *whence I came, and whither I go*; but ye know not whence I came and whither I go.

Cf. 1 *Cor.* ii. 10. But unto us God revealed them through the Spirit: for the Spirit searcheth all things, yea the deep things of God (cf. also *Eph.* v. 13).

It is more than probable that this quotation implies a knowledge of the Gospel. So clear is it that it used to be quoted as a proof of the late date of Ignatius. In *Encyclopaedia Biblica* II., 1830, Abbott suggests that it comes from Philo. But the passage he quotes has only a most distant resemblance to the one before us. And as Zahn says, the passage in Ignatius gains greatly in point when it is considered in contrast to that in St. John. Ignatius says that the Spirit itself knoweth whence it cometh and whither it goeth, clearly suggesting that there was a passage where something had been said about mankind not knowing of the Spirit whence it comes and whither it goes.

Ign. *Rom.* 7. My lust hath been crucified, and there is no fire of material longing in me, but only water living and speaking in me, saying within me, Come to the Father. I have no delight in the food of corruption or in the delights of this life. I desire the bread of God, which is the flesh of Christ, who was of the seed of David: and for a draught I desire His blood, which is love incorruptible.

Lightfoot *ad loc.* "Doubtless a reference to John iv. 10, 11, as indeed the whole passage is inspired by the Fourth Gospel."

(1) *John* iv. 10. If thou knewest the gift of God, and who it is that saith to thee, Give me to drink: thou wouldest have asked of him, and he would have given thee living water.

11. . . . From whence then hast thou that living water.

The phrase is ὕδωρ ζῶν both in the Gospel and in Ignatius.

(2) ἀρτὸν Θεοῦ. Here again is an expression taken from St. John's Gospel, vi. 33. Indeed the whole context is suggested by the question of the Evangelist's narrative. The contrast of the perishable and imperishable food, the bread and the cup as representing the flesh and blood of Christ, the mystical power emanating therefrom are all ideas contained in the context (vi. 43-59).

(3) ἀρτὸς Θεοῦ. *John* vi. 33. etc. σάρξ *John* vi. 52, etc. ἄφθαρτος. Cf. αἰώνιος. *John* vi. 40. etc.

Ign. *Magn.* 8. There is one God who *manifested* Himself through Jesus Christ His Son, who is *His word* that proceeded from silence, who in *all things* was *well-pleasing* unto Him that sent Him.

Here we have a combination of Johannine thoughts:

(1) God manifested by Jesus Christ. John xvii. 13, "And this is life eternal, that they should know thee the only true God, and him whom thou didst send, even Jesus Christ. 6. I manifested thy name unto the men," etc.

(2) The application of the word λόγος to Christ.

(3) Jesus Christ was well pleasing to Him that sent Him. John. viii. 29, I do always the things that are pleasing to Him. κατὰ παντὰ εὐηρέστησεν τῷ πέμψαντι ἀυτόν ὅτι ἐγὼ τὰ ἀρεστὰ αὐτῷ ποιῶ πάντοτε.

(4) The phrase *him that sent* is a distinctively Johannine one. It occurs constantly in St. John's Gospel and nowhere else in the N.T. v. 23. τοῦ πέμψαντος αὐτὸν, 30 τοῦ πεμψαντός με, vi. 44 θέλημα τοῦ πέμψαντός με.

(2) *The Epistles of St. John.*

Pol. 7. *For every one who shall not confess that Jesus Christ is come in the flesh is antichrist*: and whosoever shall not confess the testimony of the Cross, is of the devil; and whosoever shall pervert the oracles of the Lord to his own lusts, and say that there is neither resurrection nor judgment, that man is the first-born of Satan.

1 *John* iv. 2, 3. Every spirit which confesseth *that Jesus Christ is come in the flesh* is of God: and every spirit *which confesseth not* Jesus is not of God: and this is the spirit of the *antichrist*, whereof ye have heard that it cometh, and now it is in the world already.

2 *John* 7. For many deceivers are gone forth into the world, *even they that confess not that Jesus Christ cometh in the flesh*. This is the deceiver and the antichrist.

Most people will probably be of opinion that the resemblance is so close as to imply quotation. Abbott (*Enc. Brit.* II., 1831) thinks that Eusebius "regarded the words not as a quotation but as a mere use of Johannine traditions in vogue during the conflict against Donatism." To attribute to Eusebius such modern notions is a ludicrous anachronism, and will shew the length to which these neo-apologists can go.

Did. 10. Remember, Lord, Thy Church, to deliver it from all evil and to *perfect it in Thy love*.

1 *John* iv. 18. He that feareth is not made *perfect in love*.

The expression *to perfect in love* is sufficiently remarkable to suggest literary obligation. In the Eucharistic prayer of the Didache there are other reminiscences of Johannine thought.

There is no passage resembling the Apocalypse worth quoting.

V. *The remaining books*. Of the remaining books 1 Peter is very well attested, but of 2 Peter, James, and Jude there are no quotations worth examining.

Pol. 1. Our Lord Jesus Christ, who endured to face even death for our sins . . . *on whom, though ye saw Him not, ye believe with joy unspeakable and full of glory*.

1 *Pet*. i. 8. *Whom not having seen* ye love; on whom, though now ye see him not, yet *believing*, ye rejoice greatly *with joy unspeakable and full of glory*.

It is really difficult to believe that the somewhat striking phrase, χαρᾷ ἀνεκλαλήτῳ καὶ δεδοξασμένῃ, could be arrived at independently by two separate writers.

Pol. 2. *Wherefore girding up your loins*, serve God in fear and truth.

1 *Pet*. i. 13. *Wherefore girding up the loins* of your mind, be sober.

This is not of course a quotation on which much less stress can be laid. It may be noted that the second part of the passage in Polycarp is a reminiscence of Ps. ii. 11 (LXX.).

Pol. 2. For that ye have *believed* on Him *that raised* our Lord Jesus Christ *from the dead and gave unto Him glory*, and a throne on His right hand.

1 *Pet*. i. 21. Who through him are *believers* in God, *which raised him from the dead and gave him glory*.

Pol. 5. For it is a good thing to refrain from lust in the world, *for every lust warreth against the Spirit.*

1 *Pet.* ii. 11. Beloved, I beseech you as sojourners and pilgrims, to abstain from fleshly *lusts, which war against* the soul.

The substitution of *spirit* for *soul* comes perhaps from *Gal.* v. 17.

Pol. 10. *Having your conversation* unblameable *among the Gentiles*, that from your good works both ye may receive praise and the Lord may not be blasphemed in you.

1 *Pet.* ii. 12. *Having your conversation* honest *among the Gentiles.*

There is also in the same chapter a reminiscence of 1 *Pet.* ii. 17.

Pol. 8. Jesus Christ who *bare our sins in His own body on the tree, who did no sin, neither was guile found in His mouth*, but for our sakes He endured all things, that we might live in Him.

1 *Pet.* ii. 21. *Who did no sin, neither was guile found in his mouth.* . . .
24. *Who his own self bare our sins in his own body on the tree.*

The origin of the language of both passages is *Is.* liii. 9, 12, but Polycarp has expressions which come from 1 *Peter*.

Pol. 2. *Not rendering evil for evil, or railing for railing*, or blow for blow, or cursing for cursing.

1 *Pet.* iii. 9. *Not rendering evil for evil, or railing for railing*: but contrariwise blessing.

The striking expression also '*sober unto prayer*' (1 *Pet.* iv. 7) occurs Pol. 7.

1 Clem. 49. Love joineth us unto God; *love covereth a multitude of sins*; love endureth all things, is long suffering in all things.

1 *Pet.* iv. 8. Above all things being fervent in your love among yourselves; *for love covereth a multitude of sins.*

Clement combines with a quotation from St. Peter a reminiscence of 1 Cor. xiii. 4, 7.

The Historical Value of the Acts of the Apostles.

THE subject upon which it is my duty to speak to you to-day is one which has been much debated by scholars during the last half century, and round which an enormous literature has grown. It will only be possible to place before you the main features of the problem which presents itself, and to indicate some of the solutions which have been proposed. It may help towards a clearer understanding of the issues, if we begin by a few general considerations before we proceed to details.

(*a*) We are to discuss the *historical value* of the Acts of the Apostles, not the *inspiration* of its author. We are to regard this book as a contribution to the history of Christian origins, and we are to approach its study with an open mind, and, so far as is possible, without presuppositions. That the book was included by the early Church among canonical writings, and that it received a place in the Canon of the New Testament, so soon as the idea of a Canon was recognised, prove, indeed, that it has always been held up by the Church to the respect and veneration of her faithful members, and that it is not, in her view, merely one out of many treatises on ecclesiastical history. Like the other canonical writings, it has special title to the epithet 'inspired'; but we are beginning to recognise that the nature and limits of that inspiration are extremely hard to define, and that we are on insecure ground if we attempt to argue *a priori* from inspiration to inerrancy. We shall not, then, prejudge the question before us by making assumptions as to the degree in which inspiration guarantees historical accuracy, and we shall try to test the historical value of the Acts of the Apostles by the ordinary methods of critical enquiry. No book of the Bible is likely to suffer in our esteem, if such methods are used with honesty, sobriety, and reverence.

(*b*) Further, the question 'Is the Acts a valuable contribution to history' must not be confused with the question 'Can any errors in detail be detected in it?' No doubt, if a book were proved to contain a large number of inaccurate statements, our estimate of its historical value would be seriously impaired. But one slip in memory or one blunder in the arrangement of materials drawn from diverse sources does not destroy the authority of a modern historian; if it were so, the reputation of many great writers would be tarnished. We do not expect infallibility even from a Freeman or a Stubbs or a Lecky, while no one doubts the historical value of their work. And thus, we must not permit ourselves to think that the general authority of the Acts would disappear, if here and there it were difficult to reconcile the author's language with independent evidence for the same period. *Falsus in ūno, falsus in omnibus* may be a prudent legal maxim when the veracity of a witness is in question; it is an extremely uncritical maxim if it is applied to the credibility of a historian, whose good faith there is no reason to doubt.

(*c*) One other preliminary observation must be made. The author of the Acts believed in the possibility of what we call 'miracles'; and he records the occurrence of a considerable number, some of them of a truly remarkable character. In this he was not singular. All Christians of the early centuries, and most Christians of later centuries, have taken the same view of the *possibility*, at least, of miraculous intervention, and of the atmosphere of miracle, so to speak, by which the beginnings of Christianity were surrounded. I say nothing now as to whether this view is tenable or not—we are not met together to consider the problem of miracle; but I say that belief in God's will and power to work in ways which seem to us miraculous does not necessarily make a man an inaccurate observer or an untrustworthy historian. It may be that the author of the Acts classified as 'miraculous' some occurrences in which we, with our wider knowledge, would perceive only the operation of the ordinary laws of nature and of God; but that, if true, would only prove that he was a man of his own time and not of ours. In brief, we have no sort of title to assume that the miracle stories of the Acts are necessarily untrue; and, in the second place, the fact that the author records them without any hesitation does not put him out of court as a historian. Pascal accepted the evidence for an alleged miracle of his own day, which most of us are indisposed, I imagine, to believe—the so-called Miracle of the Holy Thorn—but he would be a bold man who would allege, therefore, that Pascal was a bad judge of evidence or an untrustworthy writer.

With these prefatory cautions, we pass to the book of the Acts. And it may be said at once that the author of this book in the form in which we have it is indisputably the author of the Third Gospel. The claim is made in the preface or dedication where the author speaks of the 'former treatise' which he had addressed to his friend, Theophilus. And the claim is amply justified by the style and language of the book which are indistinguishable from the style and language of the Gospel. "We need not stop," said Renan, "to prove this proposition which has never been seriously contested." The name of the common author has been handed down by an unbroken tradition from early times, which designates him as St. Luke, "the beloved physician," the companion and friend of St. Paul. We shall return to this point presently, but meantime we shall call him St. Luke, for convenience sake. And inasmuch as he is the author both of the Third Gospel and the Acts, a good deal that will be said of his characteristics as a historian applies alike to both books.

I. The first thing that strikes us, perhaps, when we compare St. Luke's writings with the other historical books of the New Testament, is the author's tendency to connect his narrative with the events of the contemporary history of the Roman Empire. As Zahn has pointed out, no other writer of the New Testament even names an Emperor, but St. Luke names Augustus, Tiberius, Claudius, and is at pains to date the events which he describes by the year of the Emperor's reign. We might almost say that he goes out of his way to depict the political and social environment of the Apostolic age. And he moves quite freely in describing the complicated system of government which prevailed all over the provinces. It is possible in many cases to check the accuracy of his allusions to it from the evidence which the inscriptions and the literature afford of the methods of Roman provincial administration. It has many times been pointed out, and not least successfully by our own scholars, that his accuracy is quite remarkable in details. This was fully worked out in an essay by Bishop Lightfoot, which appeared in the *Contemporary Review* for 1878, and which has since been reprinted;[1] and reference may also be made to the pages of Dr. Salmon's *Introduction to the New Testament*, which deals with the Acts. But although the topic is a well-worn one, it must not be omitted altogether, and so I mention a few examples of St. Luke's accuracy in the use of *titles*.

(*a*) He distinguishes, with the utmost precision, between the senatorial and imperial provinces of the Empire, that is, between the provinces which were governed by a Proconsul as the representative of the Senate, and those which were ruled by a Propraetor as the Emperor's viceroy. This is a matter about which mistakes could hardly be avoided by a writer who had not access to exact means of information. In times of peace a province would naturally be placed under a Proconsul, but if martial law became necessary it would be transferred to the charge of a Propraetor; and thus a province which was senatorial to-day might be imperial to-morrow. It is remarkable that St. Luke

[1] *Essays on Supernatural Religion*, p. 291 ff.

never once misapplies these titles. In Ac. xviii. 12, Gallio is rightly called Proconsul of Achaia, and in xiii. 7, Sergius Paulus is named as the Proconsul of Cyprus ; and in both cases the administration of the province had changed its character from time to time.

(*b*) Again the governor of Malta is given his correct designation, ὁ πρῶτος (Ac. xxviii. 7), the *Primus*. This is not a title that is found in literature elsewhere, and we should not be able to explain it were it not that inscriptions have been discovered at Malta which entirely confirm St. Luke's phraseology.

(*c*) Again, he knows that the magistrates at Philippi are called στρατηγοί (xvi. 20) or *praetors* ; while the magistrates at Thessalonica are given the unusual title of πολιτάρχαι (xvii. 6) or *burgomasters*. This latter designation is found in no extant author, but that it was in local use in Macedonia, and notably in Thessalonica itself, has been confirmed by the indubitable testimony of inscriptions.[1]

These considerations are of such weight that they have been recognised as noteworthy even by critics who do not count the book of the Acts to be of any special historical value. One of the most recent writers on the subject, Professor Schmiedel, who disparages the book as a whole, is constrained to admit : "After every deduction has been made,

[1] The references will be found in Dr. Knowling's full and careful commentary on the Acts in the *Expositor's Greek Testament*.

Acts certainly contains many data that are correct, as for example, especially in the matter of proper names, such as Jason, Titius Justus, Crispus, Sosthenes; or in titles, touches such as the title πολιτάρχαι, which is verified by inscriptions for Thessalonica, as is the title of πρῶτος for Malta, and probably the name of Sergius Paulus as Proconsul for Cyprus."[1]

Another point which has received a good deal of attention of recent years is the *topographical* knowledge displayed by the author, especially in connection with St. Paul's journeys through the less known parts of Asia Minor. This has been worked out by Prof. Ramsay in his interesting books, *The Church and the Roman Empire* and *St. Paul the Traveller*, to which the reader may be referred for details.

Something should now be said about the author's allusions to events of contemporary local history, which are mentioned in the pages of the Jewish historian Josephus. In three cases a particular comparison has been instituted between the notices of events in the Acts and in the *Antiquities* of Josephus; namely, the Death of Herod Agrippa (Ac. xii. 21; cp. *Antt.* xix. 8, 2), the Rebellion of the Egyptian Impostor (Ac. xxi. 38; cp. *Antt.* xx. 8, 6, B. J. II. 13, 5), and the Rising of Theudas, and subsequently of

[1] *Encycl. Biblica*, vol. i. s.v. 'Acts,' p. 47.

Judas of Galilee (Ac. v. 36 ff.; cp. *Antt.* xx. 5, 4, xviii. 1, 6, B.J. II. 8, 1 and 17, 8). Speaking in general terms, it may be said that in two of these instances, at least, the Acts and Josephus are at variance in regard to details, the number of the rebels, &c., while Josephus is not always consistent with himself. The discrepancies are not easy to reconcile, in the fragmentary condition of our knowledge of the period; but there is no ground for supposing Josephus to have been better informed than our author, if we must believe that one or other has made a mistake. One inference, however, has been drawn from these parallel narratives, which ought not to be passed by without pointing out its precarious character. It has been argued by some ingenious writers that in the pages of Josephus, who wrote about 93 A.D., we have before us the authority to which the author of Acts was indebted when he recorded the incidents in question. Were that the case, the Acts would be much later in date than has been generally believed, and it could not have been written by a contemporary of St. Paul. But, indeed, the inference will not bear investigation, and it has been rightly rejected by the best critics of all schools, by Dr. Harnack as well as by Dr. Sanday. Whatever may be thought of the relative accuracy of the Acts and Josephus in the matter of the rebellions of Theudas and of Judas, the discrepancies between the two notices are too great to permit us to believe that one copied from the other. They are quite independent.[1]

II. So much for titles, and geographical and historical allusions. For the latter part of the Acts there is, however, at hand another means of controlling St. Luke's accuracy. We are in possession of thirteen Epistles by St. Paul, of which the earlier letters were composed during circumstances described in the Acts, and in several of which there are allusions to St. Paul's movements from place to place. The argument resting on the 'undesigned coincidences' between the Acts and the Epistles put forth by Paley in the eighteenth century is not yet superseded in the main, although some details require modification; and Paley's *Horae Paulinae* may still be recommended as an introduction to the "Higher Criticism" of the New Testament. There is little doubt as to the independence of the Acts and the Pauline letters; it is indeed remarkable that the author of the Acts seems to have had no acquaintance whatever with these wonderful writings. Yet it is found that in many instances allusions in the Epistles, especially in the great controversial group of letters to the Corinthians, Romans, and Galatians, harmonise with what the Acts has to tell of the journeys and plans

[1] Comp. Mr. Headlam's article on the Acts in Hastings' *Dictionary of the Bible*, vol. I. p. 30.

of the writer. And these 'undesigned coincidences' go far to convince us of the general trustworthiness of the history. It is true that there are some difficulties in the way of reconciling Gal. i. and ii. with the Acts; but too much has been made of them. For instance, in the Acts there is no hint of St. Paul's journey to Arabia after his conversion, of which he tells in Gal. i. 17; and, again, no hint of his controversy with St. Peter at Antioch, of which he speaks with some satisfaction in Gal. ii. 11. And it is, perhaps, not quite certain whether we ought to identify St. Paul's visit to Jerusalem which he mentions in Gal. ii. 1 with the visit described in Ac. xi. 30, or with that described in Ac. xv. 4 ff., although the balance of opinion (Hort, Lightfoot, etc.) favours the latter view. But it is quite clear that St. Luke does not attempt to narrate *all* the experiences in St. Paul's eventful ministry, so that omissions need not surprise us; and, again, it is natural that he should not know as much of the earlier episodes as of the later, when he had become his friend and companion.[1]

[1] Dr. Chase, in his admirable *Hulsean Lectures* on the "Credibility of the Acts of the Apostles," which appeared since this lecture was delivered, suggests another apposite consideration. "To drag out again into the daylight all the mistakes and heartburnings of the time, if indeed St. Luke knew them, would have been a useless outrage, and he was not guilty of it. . . . The reticence of the Acts is not an argument against its veracity. . . . The tomb of dead controversies ought to be an inviolable resting-place" (p. 92).

We have now come to the point at which it is necessary for us to ask for the evidence supporting the Church's tradition that the author of the Acts was this 'Luke, the beloved physician.' I need hardly remind you that there are three sections in the later part of the Acts in which the writer uses the first person plural when telling his story. They begin according to the common text at Ac. xvi. 10.[1] After St. Paul had seen the vision of the man of Macedonia calling for help, "immediately" says the writer, "we endeavoured to go into Macedonia." The writer "appears to have joined Paul at Troas and to have accompanied him to Philippi. There he seems to have been left behind; for when Paul leaves Philippi the use of the pronoun 'we' ceases and is not resumed until Paul returns to Philippi some six or seven years later. Then (xx. 5) the 'we' begins again and continues till the arrival in Jerusalem (xxi. 18). It begins again in ch. xxvii. with St. Paul's voyage and continues until his arrival in Rome"[2] (xxviii. 16). These sections, at least, proceed from an eyewitness; their vividness of detail and exact knowledge of localities leave no room for doubt on this point. Mr. James Smith's book on the *Voyage*

[1] But in the Western text, the first person plural is used also at Ac. xi. 28; "when *we* had been gathered together," which connects the writer with the Church of Antioch.

[2] Salmon, *Introduction to N.T.*, p. 300.

and Shipwreck of St. Paul[1] supplies a most interesting and convincing commentary upon the narrative of Ac. xxvii. by one who was himself conversant with seafaring matters and who therefore spoke with authority when he pointed out the accuracy of the writer's account of the storm and the handling of the ship. This no one disputes; and the historical character of the 'We' passages of the Acts is recognised even by so destructive a critic as Schmiedel. When we ask, Who wrote this journey record? the names of Silas, Timothy, Titus have been suggested, but they are supported by no ancient authority, nor are they in themselves more likely than that of St. Luke. Indeed, St. Luke's claim has received somewhat special corroboration from the investigations of Dr. Hobart[2] and others who have found traces of medical phraseology in these, as well as in the other parts of the Acts, which would be natural if the writer were a physician, as we know St. Luke to have been.

We take St. Luke, then, as the author of the 'We' passages of the Acts, and in so doing the use of the first person plural is simply explained. But can we argue from these passages to the other parts of the book? May it not be that the author of the Acts in its present form has incorporated an authentic

[1] Dr. Breusing's *Die Nautik der Alten* goes over the same ground, and may be commended to those who can read German.

[2] *The Medical Language of St. Luke*, passim.

journey record into his narrative, which, as a whole, was composed at a later date? That is an hypothesis which cannot be dismissed off hand, and it is accepted by a good many scholars in Germany and a few in this country. But the more carefully the language of the Acts is examined, the more difficult does it seem to resist the prima facie case for the *unity* of the whole work as proceeding from one author. In the first lecture of this series,[1] Dr. Sanday referred to the careful examination of the vocabulary made by Sir John Hawkins, and to the argument based upon this, which has convinced him and others that the author of the book is identical with the writer of the 'We' passages. It is a tenable view that St. Luke incorporated in his work with alterations and additions a diary or journal in which he himself had recorded the events of which he was an eyewitness.

I have spoken of the similarity of style throughout the book, but we must be careful not to overstate our case. For it is not doubtful that there are differences, not so much in vocabulary as in tone and manner, between the earlier part of the Acts and the latter, and these differences call for more minute examination than they have hitherto received. Roughly speaking, there is a difference between the first twelve chapters and the last sixteen, which may be accounted for partly by the difference of subject

[1] P. 19 above.

matter, but which probably points also to a difference in the sources to which the writer had access. As we pass from the account of the early preaching in Jerusalem, and the period of transition while the Gospel was spreading in Judaea and Samaria, to the account of St. Paul's missionary journeys and the extension of the Gospel to the Gentiles, we feel that we have passed from Hebraism to Hellenism, from the Acts of Peter to the Acts of Paul. There is a change of atmosphere, and there is a corresponding change in the proportions of the narrative, which becomes fuller and more vivid as we proceed. That at least is the impression which is left on my own mind, and whether it be well founded or not it suggests questions as to the sources of St. Luke's narrative, which must be briefly mentioned.

We know from the Preface to the Third Gospel, and from the internal evidence of composite character which it displays, that St. Luke made use of the ordinary sources of information which a historian employs. It has been pointed out in a former lecture,[1] that he probably used two documents at least as a basis for the Gospel, and we need not be surprised, therefore, if we find that he used documents when compiling the Acts. For the latter part of the Acts, cc. xiii.-xxviii., there is not, indeed, much evidence of this, save in the case of the journal to which I have

[1] P. 12 above.

already referred. No doubt, the letter conveying the decision of the Apostolic Council at Jerusalem was many times copied, and it has probably been incorporated in its integrity in chap. xv. So, too, it is probable that the letter of Claudius Lysias to Felix (Ac. xxiii. 26 ff.) about the case of St. Paul has been exactly preserved. But in other parts the later chapters of the Acts do not suggest the use of anything like a previous narrative. The intimacy of St. Luke with his master St. Paul gave him opportunities for gaining information at first hand in respect of events of which he was not an eye-witness. But it may be asked, where did he get his report of St. Paul's speeches, which take up so large a part of the book? We have the speech at Antioch in Pisidia (xiii. 16 ff.), the speech at Athens (xvii. 22 ff.), the speech at Miletus to the Ephesian elders (xx. 18 ff.), the speech in Hebrew from the barrack steps at Jerusalem to the people (xxii. 1 ff.), the speech before Felix (xxiv. 10 ff.), and that before Agrippa (xxvi. 2 ff.). We are not bound to suppose that in every case these are fully recorded; it is more reasonable to hold that the aim of the writer was to give the substance and the more striking phrases, but not to reproduce the whole. It is true that a kind of shorthand was in fairly common use at this period, and that a formal speech like the apology before Felix might naturally have been taken down by an official reporter. But there is no probability of anything of the kind in the other cases. And only one of the speeches, that to the Ephesian elders, occurs in the "We" sections, so that we must suppose St. Luke to have had recourse to the recollections of others who heard, or of St. Paul himself who spoke. It is, then, very remarkable to find that analyses of the vocabulary betray an unusual Pauline flavour. In the speech at Athens some specially Pauline words are found; in the speech at Miletus this is even more marked; while in the apology to the Jews, which was spoken in Hebrew, while the thought is Pauline there is not a single word that is characteristic of St. Paul's Greek style. Thus, however St. Luke gained his information, he has succeeded in reporting speeches which the character of the vocabulary in every case shows to be congruous to the situation depicted.[1]

A more difficult problem remains, viz., to determine the nature of the sources, if any, from which St. Luke derived his account of the history recorded in the first twelve chapters. St. Paul may, of course, have spoken in his hearing of the incidents of his own conversion, which are, however, told from a somewhat different angle in his speeches in cc. xxii., xxvi. And it has been suggested that while St. Luke was at Caesarea (cc. xxi. 7, xxiv.-xxvi.) he may have

[1] Comp. Salmon, *Introduction to N.T.*, p. 316 ff.

learnt a good deal from Philip the Evangelist, who lived there, of the early fortunes of the Church. The story of the Ethiopian eunuch (in c. viii.), and the story of Cornelius and St. Peter (in cc. x., xi.) might well have been told to him by St. Philip. But just as in the case of the Gospel the hypothesis of oral tradition seems insufficient for the phenomena it presents, so is it with the Acts. Something has been already said of the difference of tone and accent in the earlier and later chapters of the Acts, and it seems most likely that this difference is to be accounted for by presupposing the use, for the early chapters, of some primitive records of the Church at Jerusalem.[1] I would disclaim any sympathy with elaborate theories of dissection, which profess to distinguish the various sources employed at every point. Clemen, for instance, finds four sources in all, viz., a History of the Hellenists, a History of St. Peter, a History of St. Paul, and the Journal containing the 'We' sections, upon which he supposes three editors in succession to have worked. That is too ingenious to be convincing, and I do not dwell upon it. But to urge that we may distinguish the two parts of the book from each other, the one being Hebraic and the other Hellenic in tone, both being worked over with skill and judgment by St. Luke, is much more plausible.

[1] Comp. what is said on p. 18 above of one theory as to the nature of the "source" for Ac. i.-xii.

Let me shortly indicate one or two of the more conspicuous features of these early chapters:[1]

(*a*) The language used in the speeches of St. Peter about our Lord is quite clearly primitive, and entirely consonant to what the probabilities of the case would suggest. The Christology of these early chapters bases itself consistently on the fulfilment of prophecy. Jesus is the Christ who was to come, as is demonstrated by His resurrection. That is the burden of the Apostolic teaching. 'Christ' is used as a title rather than as a personal name. And He is called the 'Servant of God' (iii. 13, 26; iv. 27, 30), a phrase which we meet nowhere else in the N.T., but which goes back to the prophecies of the later Isaiah. All this is quite unlike St. Paul's language, although, of course, it is entirely harmonious with it in substance. The Christianity of these early chapters is Judaic Christianity.

(*b*) So, too, is the Church organisation incomplete and primitive. Christianity is still conceived of by the first disciples as a reformed Judaism; the temple services and the synagogue worship are still thankfully and habitually used. There has been no break with Judaism, such as came at a later time.

(*c*) The actual phraseology of the speeches, as

[1] Reference may now be made to the very full and clear discussion of the speeches of St. Peter, provided by Dr. Chase in his third Hulsean Lecture.

well as of the narrative sections, seems to betray a Hebrew or an Aramaic base. We have to reckon, indeed, with the possibility that the Semitic turns of phrase which met us here are due, not to an underlying document, but to the form which, at a very early period, the Christian tradition assumed in oral teaching. Dalman, who has special claims to be heard on such a point, warns us that "it is thus *possible* that the oldest Christian writing may have been composed in Greek; and its Semitisms, so far as they are Biblicisms, are in that case due to the Aramaic oral archetype of the Christian tradition."[1] It is clear, therefore, that we cannot yet speak with absolute confidence as to the inferences to be derived from the Semitisms of the early chapters of *Acts*; but it is equally clear that, however we are to explain them, they are more conspicuously present in the text than is the case in the later chapters of the same book. I may be permitted to express my own belief that the hypothesis of an underlying Semitic document affords at once the readiest and the most complete explanation of the facts.

These features of the early chapters show at any rate that we have in the writer of the Acts a man who had access to excellent sources of information, and was, moreover, endowed with a quite extraordinary sense of historical perspective. There are no anachronisms

[1] Dalman, *The Words of Jesus* (Engl. Tr.), p. 71.

that we can detect. And this is the more remarkable when we find that many popular manuals of early Jewish Christianity, which are published at the present day, betray a lack of this historical sense of growth and proportion which the writer of the Acts so perfectly displays.

But, supposing that St. Luke had access to some primitive records of the Church at Jerusalem, how did he use them? Did he incorporate them bodily into his work, or did he only use them for facts, and not at all for phrases? Did he combine information derived from different sources? or did he copy without alteration what lay before him? These questions—or some of them—cannot be answered with confidence until the researches which are being pursued as to the structure of the third gospel are much further advanced. When we know how and with what freedom St. Luke used his documentary materials for his former treatise we shall be in a better position for forming an opinion about his later treatise. It has been suggested that in compiling his gospel St. Luke's habit was to take sections of considerable length, now from one source, now from another, and to piece them together. If this were so with the Gospel it may have been so with the Acts. But in any case it is quite certain that St. Luke *edited* his materials. He worked them over, he introduced his own favourite words and turns of phrase, and thus imparted to his work a unity which a product of scissors and paste could never possess. We must not lose sight of this. It was not without reason that Renan called the third gospel 'the most beautiful book in the world.'[1] For St. Luke has the characteristics of a really good writer. He has remarkable command of words, and he has—what is less common—tact and taste in the selection of the incidents which he embodies in his narratives. He is not a mere chronicler, but a historian who writes with a plan and a purpose. That plan in the Acts is not so crude as those think who have persuaded themselves that the main object of the writer is to draw out a parallel between St. Peter and St. Paul. Remarkable parallels may be traced, without doubt, between the careers of these two great Apostles, as recorded in the Acts; but they are not more numerous or more striking than might be anticipated between the careers of any two men trying to do the same work under somewhat similar circumstances. With much more truth—though it would not be the whole truth—might it be said that St. Luke aims at tracing the progress of the Gospel from Jerusalem outward, until it reaches Rome, and that his 'tendency'—if he has a tendency—is to justify to Jew and Greek the Gentile Christianity which gradually but surely replaced the Jewish Christianity of early days. We do not know with certainty the date of the composition

[1] *Les Evangiles*, p. 283.

of the Acts ; some writers of repute place it before the year 70. I should not care to express an opinion with full confidence ; but I am disposed rather to agree with those (*e.g.* Harnack and Sanday) who think that both Gospel and Acts were written after the Fall of Jerusalem ; and that thus we may reckon the Acts to have been published about A.D. 80. Jerusalem had fallen ; the hopes of Judaism were shattered. But a new hope had arisen for the world ; and the last verse of the Acts looks out with something of joyous expectation to the future of the Church. It leaves the Apostle of the Gentiles, the champion of freedom at Rome, "preaching the kingdom of God and teaching those things which concern the Lord Jesus Christ with all confidence, no man forbidding him" (Ac. xxviii. 36).

GLASGOW: PRINTED AT THE UNIVERSITY PRESS BY ROBERT MACLEHOSE AND CO.